Effective Learning Activities

Chris Dickinson

Published by Network Educational Press Ltd
PO Box 635
Stafford
ST16 1BF

First Published 1996
Reprinted 1998, 2000
© Chris Dickinson 1996

ISBN 1 85539 035 3

Series Editor - Professor Tim Brighouse
Edited by Sara Fielding
Design & layout by Neil Gordon
Cover design by Neil Hawkins of Devine Design
Illustrations by Joe Rice

Printed in Great Britain by
Redwood Books, Trowbridge, Wilts.

Acknowledgements

Many people have unknowingly contributed to this book.
Thanks must go to the hundreds of teachers who, during INSET,
have questioned and probed my understanding. In trying to
explain myself, I have come to better understand.

Three people need particular thanks, for without
them this book would not exist.

Four years working with Rob Powell in Network Consultancy
gave me access to a source of constant stimulation and advice
about what learning can look like in classrooms.

Barbara Teale of South Gloucestershire LEA provided
very necessary encouragement and many
examples of good practice.

Sara Fielding ensured the book was written on
time and then gave me the professional feedback
necessary to ensuring it could be read.

Chris Dickinson
June 1996

The School Effectiveness Series

Foreword

A teacher's task is much more ambitious than it used to be and demands a focus on the subtleties of teaching and learning and on the emerging knowledge of school improvement.

This is what this series is about.

Teaching can be a very lonely activity. The time honoured practice of a single teacher working alone in the classroom is still the norm; yet to operate alone is, in the end, to become isolated and impoverished. This series addresses two issues - the need to focus on practical and useful ideas connected with teaching and learning and the wish thereby to provide some sort of an antidote to the loneliness of the long distance teacher who is daily berated by an anxious society.

Teachers flourish best when, in key stage teams or departments (or more rarely whole schools), their talk is predominantly about teaching and learning and where, unconnected with appraisal, they are privileged to observe each other teach; to plan and review their work together; and to practise the habit of learning from each other new teaching techniques. But how does this state of affairs arise? Is it to do with the way staffrooms are physically organised so that the walls bear testimony to interesting articles and in the corner there is a dedicated computer tuned to 'conferences' about SEN, school improvement, the teaching of English etc, and whether, in consequence, the teacher leaning over the shoulder of the enthusiastic IT colleagues sees the promise of interesting practice elsewhere? Has the primary school cracked it when it organises successive staff meetings in different classrooms and invites the 'host' teacher to start the meeting with a 15 minute exposition of their classroom organisation and management? Or is it the same staff sharing, on a rota basis, a slot on successive staff meeting agenda when each in turn reviews a new book they have used with their class? And what of the whole school which now uses 'active' and 'passive' concerts of carefully chosen music as part of their accelerated learning techniques?

It is of course well understood that excellent teachers feel threatened when first they are observed. Hence the epidemic of trauma associated with OFSTED. The constant observation of the teacher in training seems like that of the learner driver. Once you have passed your test and can drive unaccompanied, you do. You often make lots of mistakes and sometimes get into bad habits. Woe betide, however, the back seat driver who tells you so. In the same way the new teacher quickly loses the habit of observing others and being observed. So how do we get a confident, mutual observation debate going? One school I know found a simple and therefore brilliant solution. The Head of the History Department asked that a young colleague plan lessons for her - the Head of Department - to teach. This lesson she then taught and was observed by the young colleague. The subsequent discussion, in which the young teacher asked:

> *"Why did you divert the question and answer session I had planned?"*

and was answered by,

> *"Because I could see that I needed to arrest the attention of the group by the window with some hands on role play, etc."*

lasted an hour and led to a once-a-term repeat discussion which, in the end, was adopted by the whole school. The whole school subsequently changed the pattern of its meetings to consolidate extended debate about teaching and learning. The two teachers claimed that because one planned and the other taught both were implicated but neither alone was responsible or felt 'got at'.

So there are practices which are both practical and more likely to make teaching a rewarding and successful activity. They can, as it were, increase the likelihood of a teacher surprising the pupils into understanding or doing something they did not think they could do rather than simply entertaining them or worse still occupying them. There are ways of helping teachers judge the best method of getting pupil expectation just ahead of self-esteem.

This series focuses on straightforward interventions which individual schools and teachers use to make life more rewarding for themselves and those they teach. Teachers deserve nothing less for they are the architects of tomorrow's society and society's ambition for what they achieve increases as each year passes.

Professor Tim Brighouse.

Contents

Section One   Introduction   1

Section Two   Advanced Organisers   13

Section Three   White Space   25

Section Four   Separate Resources   31

Section Five   Vocabulary & Prompts   37

Section Six   Variety of Products   47

Section Seven   Getting Started   57

Section Eight   Resources   61

Index   63

INTRODUCTION

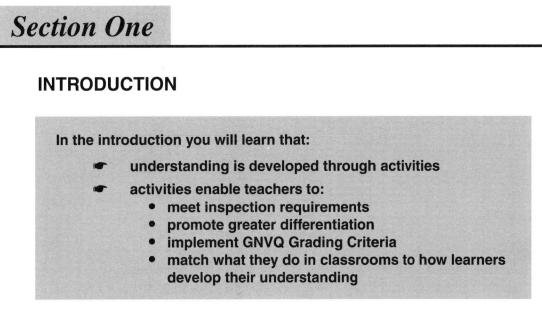

In the introduction you will learn that:

☞ **understanding is developed through activities**

☞ **activities enable teachers to:**
- **meet inspection requirements**
- **promote greater differentiation**
- **implement GNVQ Grading Criteria**
- **match what they do in classrooms to how learners develop their understanding**

Whilst this book relies heavily on educational theory and research, it is intended to be practical. Quotations and references will point the interested reader to the relevant research. The sections here, however, do build into a framework for the construction of effective learning activities. We all feel the need to re-invent the wheel. Sometimes it just helps to know that 'round with spokes' is useful.

Let's start by considering the following worksheet which is fairly typical of the worksheets that teachers spend much time producing. Now ask yourself, what have the students got written in their files or exercise books once they have finished?

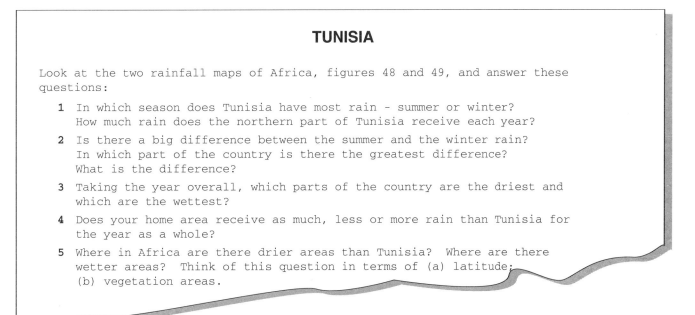

TUNISIA

Look at the two rainfall maps of Africa, figures 48 and 49, and answer these questions:

1 In which season does Tunisia have most rain - summer or winter?
   How much rain does the northern part of Tunisia receive each year?

2 Is there a big difference between the summer and the winter rain?
   In which part of the country is there the greatest difference?
   What is the difference?

3 Taking the year overall, which parts of the country are the driest and which are the wettest?

4 Does your home area receive as much, less or more rain than Tunisia for the year as a whole?

5 Where in Africa are there drier areas than Tunisia? Where are there wetter areas? Think of this question in terms of (a) latitude; (b) vegetation areas.

It is not difficult to see what is happening here. The writer has a clear expectation of the knowledge to be acquired by the learner. This worksheet mainly requires the learner to move information from one place to another and, as such, reflects a view of teaching and learning which is largely concerned with the transmission of facts to learners.

Inspection evidence is calling into question the efficacy of this approach. *The Annual Report of Her Majesty's Chief Inspector of Schools 1994/95* (**HMSO, 1996**) makes frequent reference to the disparity between pupils being able to transmit facts, but not being able to demonstrate understanding.

In Science KS3/4 for instance:

> *Pupils are generally able to record measurements in an organised way, to draw graphs and to analyse these where relationships are simple. The abilities required to make predictions based on relevant scientific knowledge and to evaluate the outcomes of the investigation are often less well developed.*
>
> *(Page 22)*

In History KS3/4:

> *Where standards fall short... it is often because teachers limit the depth of pupils' investigations by asking too many closed questions...*
>
> *(Page 28)*

In KS3 Modern Foreign Languages:

> *Pupils work conscientiously and accurately on tasks such as copywriting, gap filling, writing answers to written questions or adapting dialogues on transactional topics. Opportunities are rare however, for pupils to undertake sustained writing using memorised language about, for example, personal interests and hobbies or projects such as creating a brochure to attract foreign visitors to their town. When they do occur, pupils often write enthusiastically at some length and are able to deploy effectively a wider range of structure and vocabulary.*
>
> *(Page 29)*

Finally, the gap between knowing and understanding is apparently at its most acute in GNVQ courses:

> *Work of a high standard is, however, uncommon. Much of the work in students' portfolios shows that they can plan activities and gather information. They produce sufficient evidence to show knowledge of vocational areas and are able to meet the specified GNVQ requirements. However, their understanding of key concepts is variable and their ability to analyse critically and evaluate is often too limited.*
>
> *Much of the poorer work is linked to inadequate, undemanding tasks often based on summarising information from textbooks. Frequently this arises from an excessive emphasis on the coverage required by the course with too little attention devoted to securing an appropriate depth of understanding or level of skill.*
>
> *(Page 35)*

Whilst these comments reflect conclusions drawn from inspections in 1994/95 they are neither particularly new nor original.

> *... many teachers see teaching primarily as an act of transmitting existing knowledge, minimising the part actively played by pupils... Teaching in which transmission predominates is the negation of education for living.*
>
> *(D Barnes, From Communication to Curriculum, Penguin 1975)*

In *'From Communication to Curriculum'*, a critical milestone in our understanding of how learners construct meaning, Douglas Barnes raises several questions about this transmission mode of learning.

> *If in the classroom we limit written language to getting information from a book and writing it down to show the teacher that the work is done, we ignore and reject its function as an instrument for reshaping experience, that is, as a means of learning.*
>
> *Both the traditional teacher-dominated lesson and the mode of working implied by worksheets are based upon an implicit distrust of children's ability to learn.*
>
> *Many teachers see knowledge as the possession of trained adults...(but) even when a trained adult has formulated...a series of statements...these...remain no more than marks upon paper until learners have worked upon it themselves, and related it to what they already know.*
>
> *(D Barnes, op. cit)*

The questions raised by Barnes challenge the view that understanding comes from acquisition. We can acquire a piece of information without necessarily understanding it. For example, a pupil may know about monetary theory and be able to work through routine questions in the textbook, but it does not necessarily follow that the pupil understands the theory. If, on the other hand, the pupil could, in the context of a class debate, argue for a reduction in interest rates we might be more ready to accept that the pupil understands. Understanding goes beyond knowing. This view is a recurrent theme of educationalists:

> *Following the traditional view of knowledge...the teacher...will tend to ask essentially closed questions, expecting students to reproduce the facts or ideas previously presented... The alternative conception implies the asking of open questions... The students are then encouraged to see learning as a reorganisation and transformation of their understanding of aspects of the real world.*
>
> *(Marton, et al., The Experience of Learning, Scottish Academic Press, 1984)*

Indeed, it became a view also held by HMI:

> *Pupils learn most effectively when they are actively involved in tasks which provide first-hand experience of practical skills and require recording, reporting or an imaginative response.*
> *(HM Inspectors of Schools (SOED), Effective Primary Schools, HMSO 1989)*

The common ground in these quotations is the emphasis they place on performance. The assertion that learners have to 'perform their understanding' underpins the work of Project Zero at Harvard Graduate School of Education and, in particular the collaboration of researchers at Harvard with teachers in the Boston area in the 'Teaching for Understanding Project'. David Perkins and Tina Blythe (*'Putting Understanding Up Front,* **Educational Leadership**', **February 1994**) outline a performance model for understanding which states that understanding is a matter of being able to do a variety of thought-demanding things with a topic, such as explaining, finding evidence and examples, generalizing, analogizing, and representing the topic in a new way.

The framework that they and co-workers have developed highlights four key concepts:

1	**Topics should be generative**, that is they should be: a) central to the discipline, b) accessible to students, c) connectable to other diverse topics.
2	**Goals should be specified in terms of understanding,** e.g. "By the end of this unit students will understand that..."
3	**Teachers design 'understanding performances'** that is, tasks that allow students to show that they understand. Ultimately, students might develop some 'culminating' performance of understanding such as an extended essay or an exhibition.
4	**Ongoing assessment**. To learn for understanding, students need criteria, feedback and opportunities for reflection from the beginning of and throughout any sequence of instruction.

With this emphasis on performance, understanding becomes much more active. In order to understand we have to do more than acquire information; we have to process, we have to do something with it. Understanding comes from usage not acquisition. Recent work in the United Kingdom lends support to this assertion.

> *ALIS (A Level Information Service, University of Newcastle) survey data has shown that better than expected exam results have been generally associated with more frequent use of student presentations - not just in one set of data but over three consecutive years.*
> *(Students at the Front: A successful teaching strategy at A Level. Unpublished article by Carol Fitzgibbon, 1992)*

Within the framework outlined by Project Zero what we see are A Level students 'performing their understanding' with evidence to suggest that this improves results. Similarly, when researching small, mixed ability, group work in science, Christine Howe of Strathclyde University found that when pupils discussed their work collaboratively, "the pupils with relatively good science knowledge progressed as much as the pupils with relatively poor." (**SCRE** '*Research in Education*' *No. 55,* **Autumn 1994**)

In both these examples we see students deepening and consolidating their understanding through the performance of that understanding. As they work to make meaning for others, they make meaning for themselves. In the light of this 'performance model' consider the following two examples of activities devised for Key Stage Three students.

Not all the information available to the students is presented here. Only the central activities which illustrate the performance of understanding are quoted.

EXAMPLE 1
MATHEMATICS:

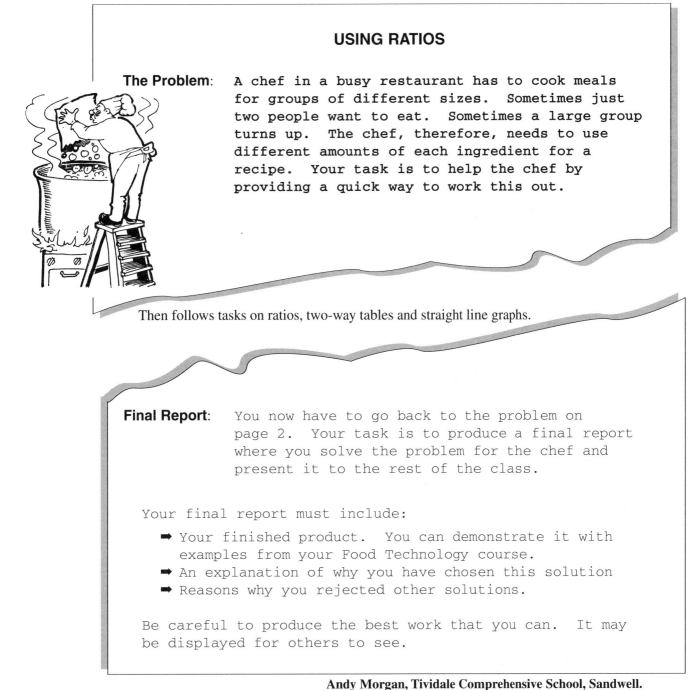

USING RATIOS

The Problem: A chef in a busy restaurant has to cook meals for groups of different sizes. Sometimes just two people want to eat. Sometimes a large group turns up. The chef, therefore, needs to use different amounts of each ingredient for a recipe. Your task is to help the chef by providing a quick way to work this out.

Then follows tasks on ratios, two-way tables and straight line graphs.

Final Report: You now have to go back to the problem on page 2. Your task is to produce a final report where you solve the problem for the chef and present it to the rest of the class.

Your final report must include:

➡ Your finished product. You can demonstrate it with examples from your Food Technology course.
➡ An explanation of why you have chosen this solution
➡ Reasons why you rejected other solutions.

Be careful to produce the best work that you can. It may be displayed for others to see.

Andy Morgan, Tividale Comprehensive School, Sandwell.
Terry Parker, Churchdown School, Gloucester.

Effective Learning Activities

EXAMPLE 2
MODERN LANGUAGES:

Margin notes

Situation

On recherche un groupe de jeunes pour préparer la campagne de publicité pour un nouveau restaurant, Le Chat noir. Ton groupe est invité à présenter des idées.

Possibilites

➤ une publicité pour la radio
➤ une feuille de publicité pour distribuer dans la rue
➤ des menus
➤ un article pour un journal local

Network Educational Press Ltd

This performance model sits well with a number of current important concerns which are raising the concept of understanding higher up the agenda. In addition, new theories about the psychology of learning point in the same direction. It is possible, therefore, to consider pressures for teaching for understanding as coming from four key areas:

- the OFSTED framework for inspection
- the need for greater differentiation
- the implementation of GNVQ
- the work of Howard Gardner on multiple intelligence

OFSTED FRAMEWORK FOR INSPECTION

The framework for the inspection of schools, introduced in April 1996, sets out in section 5.1 the importance of understanding. Outlining the basis for judgement, reference is made to:

1) the extent to which teachers set high expectations so as to challenge pupils and deepen their understanding.

2) planning activities and carrying them out.

3) an ability to draw on a range of contexts and resources to make subject knowledge comprehensible to pupils.

4) in terms of expectations, how teachers make clear the importance of the use of critical thinking, creativity and imagination.

Specifically, in relation to methods and strategies to meet curricular objectives and the needs of pupils, inspectors are required to have evidence of this judged by the extent to which the methods used, amongst other things:

- are based on what pupils know, understand and can do and what they need to know next.
- provide for questioning which probes pupils' knowledge and understanding and challenges thinking.

- provides for practical activity which is purposeful and encourages pupils to think about what they are doing and what they have learned, including how to improve.
- includes investigations and problem-solving to help pupils to apply and extend their learning in new contexts.

It is possible to see within this framework, elements of a performance model of understanding. It is also possible to see that the worksheet at the head of this section would give little opportunity for pupils to deepen their understanding, nor for the generation of evidence to satisfy the criteria set out in the framework for inspection.

In the example which follows we can see children being given the opportunity to:

- plan and carry out activities
- solve problems
- think creatively and imaginatively
- extend their learning into new contexts

As well as being given the chance to:

- select and use relevant resources and work together in lessons (OFSTED Framework section 4.2, Attitudes, Behaviour and Personal Development).

**EXAMPLE 3
SCIENCE:**

In short, they are asked to perform their understanding.

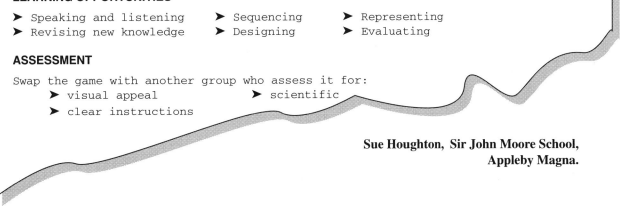

MAKING A FOREST DETECTIVE GAME

Teacher's notes

CONTEXT: Follow up to a forest visit where the activity leader had taken us on a forest detective trail looking for clues to where animals had been.

AIM: To understand that habitats give clues as to the animal populations that occupy them.

METHOD: The children (Yr 6) work in small groups (3 or 4). They follow the following task list:

1. Make a list of clues
2. Make a list of animals
3. Talk about and decide what you have to do to win your game
4. Decide on how the animal clues are going to be used
5. Decide on the layout of your board
6. Make a list of playing pieces, cards and anything else you need to play your game
7. Divide out the work and decide who will make what. Make sure that you've all agreed on sizes so that it will all fit together

When you've finished your bit, see if anyone else would like some help. Now you have made it, have a game. Was it alright? If anything needs changing do it now. Lastly, as a group, write down the rules and instructions.

LEARNING OPPORTUNITIES

- Speaking and listening
- Revising new knowledge
- Sequencing
- Designing
- Representing
- Evaluating

ASSESSMENT

Swap the game with another group who assess it for:
- visual appeal
- clear instructions
- scientific

**Sue Houghton, Sir John Moore School,
Appleby Magna.**

Effective Learning Activities

THE NEED FOR GREATER DIFFERENTIATION

Identifying the importance of differentiation in March 1990, the National Curriculum Council gave the following pointers towards a practical definition:

> **The National Curriculum will help teachers to:**
>
> - assess what each pupil knows, understands and can do
> - use their assessments and programmes of study to identify the learning needs of individual pupils
> - plan programmes of work which take account of their pupils' attainment and allow them to work at different levels
> - ensure that all pupils achieve their maximum potential.

Again reference is made to understanding and the interesting as well as problematic area of maximising potential. Evidence presented to a DES Invitation Conference on Able Pupils and the National Curriculum in April 1990 set out nine requirements that very bright pupils had identified, which provide clues to the kind of provision that best meets their needs and allows them to maximise their potential.

It was found that able pupils:

- care more about teachers' comments than about grades
- want comments to be truthful, realistic and challenging
- enjoy doing research
- employ sophisticated learning techniques
- do not enjoy being given projects to do, but want a broader brief with clear parameters
- hate purposeless copying and repeating
- do not wish to be separated as a group, but want to be challenged by peers of equal ability
- want time to talk to the teacher
- are serious about work and want it to be constructively criticised

What is clear from this list is that able pupils themselves wish to be challenged and that in large measure they wish this to be through dialogue with the teacher. Of further interest is the apparent notion that able pupils wish to be challenged within the curriculum rather than by special provision outside it. Indeed, special provision for able pupils either by withdrawal or through extra curricular clubs raises three problems in addition to the fact that they, themselves, don't wish to be separated:

- the activities can become isolated experiences which are totally unrelated to a pupil's mainstream education
- equality of opportunity issues are raised in that all pupils can benefit greatly from enrichment
- able children can hide their ability so as not to be treated differently

The issue for teachers, therefore, in making provision for able children is how to do so through approaches to teaching and learning within the classroom (see *'Effective Provision for Able & Talented Children'*, **Network Educational Press Ltd**. for more information on this subject). A similar issue is raised by the Special Educational Need Code of Practice introduced in 1994. Stage 1 of the Code of Practice is characterised by the initial identification and registration of the child's special educational need. It involves:

1. gathering of basic information about the child
2. taking early action to meet the child's needs within normal classroom work
3. monitoring and reviewing the child's progress

It becomes the child's class teacher or form tutor's responsibility to identify ways in which increased differentiation in classroom work might better meet the needs of the child.

A danger can emerge in relation to differentiation where the focus is on special educational need in the narrow sense of that phrase. Often at the forefront of teacher's minds is the demand for success. Aware of the requirement to build self-esteem, activities can be set which enable pupils to achieve success, but which are hardly challenging. Defining differentiation in 1993 in relation to science teaching, the National Curriculum Council stated simply that it is the matching of work to the abilities of individual children, so that they are stretched, but still achieve success. It is challenge with success that builds self-esteem whereas success without challenge can leave children feeling patronised. This connection between self-esteem and achievement is quite crucial.

> **The connection between behaviour and self-esteem is well documented, but research is now showing that the correlation between self-esteem and school achievement is as high as that between IQ and school achievement... Self-esteem is the pivotal point between success and failure; it has a marked effect on learning.**
> *(M. White, Self-Esteem, Daniels Publishing, 1991)*

Again the issue becomes how to make provision for children with special educational needs through the approaches to teaching and learning within the classroom. In the following example from an Avon secondary school an activity has been designed that not only enables students to 'perform their understanding', but also enables differentiation to take place within the one activity by providing opportunities for different entry points. Self-esteem is not threatened by being given easy work to do and able students are not treated differently.

**EXAMPLE 4
ENGLISH:**

PERSONAL RESEARCH PROJECT ON ANIMALS

AIMS

For you to be able to research a controversial topic and show that you can:

➤ Locate information
➤ Read and re-read information
➤ Understand facts and opinions expressed
➤ Publish your work as a double page feature in a teenage magazine
➤ Talk about your work to the class

CHOOSE A TOPIC TO RESEARCH

There are many ideas listed below. It is important to choose an area that you think you will be able to find information on.

TOPIC IDEAS

➤ Hunting animals - deer, foxes, hares, badgers
➤ Animal experiments - testing drugs, testing cosmetics
➤ Hunting - whales, trapping, fur, luxury clothes, animals for trophies
➤ Cruel sports - bullfighting, dog baiting
➤ Cruelty on the farm - misery in cattle butchery,

THE IMPLEMENTATION OF GNVQ

In 1988, HMI were critical of teaching and learning styles post-16. In more than half the lessons seen in sixth forms, students spent a considerable proportion of their time as passive recipients of information, little opportunity was provided for discussion or the interchange of ideas and they undertook little independent reading and lacked appropriate study strategies. On many occasions the style of teaching - lecture presentations, the dictation of copious notes and the practice of examination answers - left hardly any scope for students to participate.

It was also argued that not much had changed since 1979, so it would appear that there was a dominant approach to teaching and learning post-16 which was characterised by the transmission of information. The Chief Inspector's Annual Report as we have seen, suggests this still applies for GNVQ yet such an approach, applied to GNVQ, would not allow students to maximise their potential and, therefore, creates greater pressure to move to a performance model. The grading criteria for GNVQ are arranged into four themes:

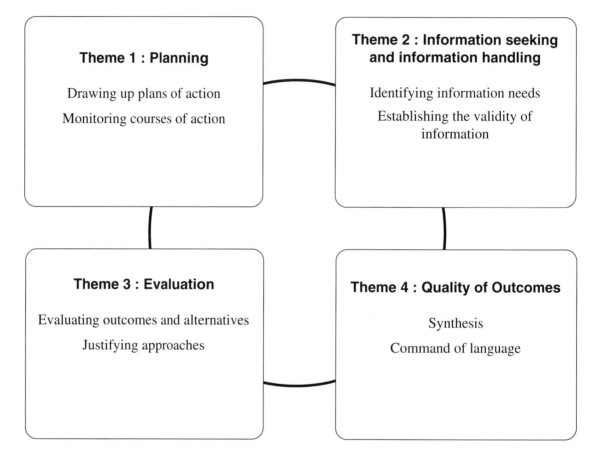

Theme 1 : Planning

Drawing up plans of action

Monitoring courses of action

Theme 2 : Information seeking and information handling

Identifying information needs

Establishing the validity of information

Theme 3 : Evaluation

Evaluating outcomes and alternatives

Justifying approaches

Theme 4 : Quality of Outcomes

Synthesis

Command of language

With the exception of Theme 4, the grading criteria are based on process skills rather than knowledge of content. To put this another way, whether a student achieves a pass, merit or distinction at GNVQ is based not so much on their handling or mastery of content as on their approach to work and the processes they go through in generating the work that goes into their portfolio of evidence. It is, therefore, the nature of the grading criteria at GNVQ which generates the pressure for a performance model of understanding.

In the following example, GNVQ students are able to demonstrate their knowledge, skills and understanding as well as use of core skills in the production of a piece of work for their portfolio. The 'performance of understanding' requires planning, information seeking and information handling. As with other units the students would be expected to carry out subsequent evaluation.

EXAMPLE 5
GNVQ
BUSINESS:

INVESTIGATING MARKETING IDEAS

> Your final task is to develop and present an outline of the marketing mix for a new product which Fizz could now launch.

Areas to research

You will present your possible product prototype, with packaging and suitable promotional material, to a Board Meeting. In your presentation you should cover the marketing mix of:

- product range development
- price
- packaging
- promotions
- sales distribution
- customer service.

Presentation

If possible, prepare packaging examples and promotional material using DTP equipment. As you prepare your presentation you will need to consider:

- the guidelines of the Trading Standards Authority and Adverti Standards Authority (you may need to research thi
- the ethics (integrity and hone may be ques

Network Educational Press Ltd

HOWARD GARDNER AND MULTIPLE INTELLIGENCE

In recent years, knowledge of the workings of the brain has begun to have an impact on approaches to teaching and learning. (See 'Accelerated Learning in the Classroom', the first book in this series for a more detailed examination of this topic.) One of the most influential writers in this field is Howard Gardner, Co-Director of Project Zero and Professor of Neurology at the Boston University School of Medicine. In 'Frames of Mind' (**Basic Books, 1993**) Gardner concludes that we don't just have one intelligence, we have seven:

1. Linguistic intelligence — *the ability to speak and write well*
2. Logical-mathematical intelligence — *the ability to reason, calculate and think logically*
3. Visual-spatial intelligence — *the ability to paint, draw and sculpt*
4. Bodily-kinesthetic intelligence — *the ability to use one's hands and body*
5. Musical intelligence — *the ability to compose, play an instrument or sing*
6. Interpersonal intelligence — *the ability to relate well to others*
7. Intrapersonal intelligence — *the ability to know oneself*

It is not difficult to see that, according to Gardner's classification, traditional teaching methods work through, and aim at, developing only two of these intelligences; linguistic and logical-mathematical. With this narrow focus, potential is limited, since our ability to understand and make sense of the world comes through exercising all seven intelligences. Indeed the ALIS findings and the conclusions of Christine Howe of Strathclyde University can both be attributed to the role of interpersonal intelligence. Again this points to a performance model of understanding. Gardner's perspective provides a neurophysiological explanation of why understanding comes from usage rather than acquisition and provides a framework for thinking of the many forms that usage can take:

- a verbal explanation to someone else   - linguistic intelligence
- a flow diagram   - logical-mathematical
- a mind map (cf. Tony Buzan)   - visual spatial
- a role play   - bodily-kinesthetic
- a jingle   - musical
- a discussion   - interpersonal
- an individual action plan   - intrapersonal

In conclusion, therefore:

- understanding is not the same as knowing
- understanding requires performance
- the performance of understanding can best be achieved through activities
- activities can meet OFSTED criteria, provide for differentiation and enable GNVQ students to achieve merits and distinctions
- through activities we can make use of more of our intelligences

Example 6
Religious Education:

ISLAM
THE FIVE PILLARS RAP

Pillar number <u>one</u> we call Shahadah
We believe in God and we call him Allah.

Salah's number <u>two</u> 'cause we like to pray
kneeling on our mats five times a day.

Zakah is number <u>three</u> 'cause we like to care
A percentage of our wealth we willingly share.

For pillar number <u>four</u> (Saum) we go on a fast
For as long as the month of Ramadan lasts.

Then comes Hajj that's pillar number <u>five</u>
We'll travel to Mecca while we're alive.

Being a Muslim is important you see
'Cause we're part of a worldwide family.

RE Department, Denny High School, Falkirk.

With the points in this introduction in mind, let's return to the worksheet on Tunisia and now consider the following alternative:

Advanced Organisers (Section 2)

TUNISIA

A group of archeologists are due to visit Tunisia and have asked you to advise them about its climate. Your task is to prepare some kind of document or presentation which gives them all the facts they need.

You may use any of the resources listed on page 2. Your document/ presentation should include the following sections:

Separate Resources (Section 4)

1. Rainfall - include details on:
   how much rain; regional differences; seasonal differences; wettest and driest regions

2. Comparisons with UK and other parts of Africa - include details on rainfall compared with where you live; drier and wetter parts of Africa in terms of latitude and vegetation

Variety of Products (Section 6)

Provided you include the above information, your presentation could be:

Vocabulary and Prompts (Section 5)

- written (a report, handwritten or wordprocessed; a letter; a script of an imaginary telephone conversation)
- spoken (a presentation; a cassette tape; a 'question time' event)
- visual (a poster; annotated map; computer graphics)
- multi media.

Use this space to record data

White Space (Section 3)

Network Consultancy

The annotations provide the section headings for the rest of the book.

ADVANCED ORGANISERS

In this section you will learn that:

☞ **advanced organisers improve the quality of work and time on task**

☞ **right-brain learners need a big picture**

☞ **there are six ways of providing an advanced organiser:**

- **The question comes first**
- **Putting the summary at the begining**
- **Giving a structured template**
- **Providing a note-taking matrix**
- **Mapping the mind**
- **Going to the future base**

In the outline of the 'performance model' presented in the previous section, reference was made to framing goals in term of understanding, e.g. *"By the end of this unit pupils will understand that..."* The point of such a list of understanding goals is to give focus to the teaching and learning. There is nothing new here, at least not in terms of outlining goals. For at least two generations teachers have been setting out aims and objectives for their schemes of work. What may be new is the importance that is now attached to learners being clearly aware of the aims and objectives of the work they are undertaking.

As early as 1960, the cognitive psychologist, Ausubel drew our attention to the importance of the 'advanced organiser'. Whilst advanced organisers can take many forms, essentially they are models, provided in advance of the main learning task, that help learners to sort and classify the content to be learnt.

It is now widely held that the provision of an advanced organiser is directly related to:

1 The quality of work done

2 Time on task (the percentage time in a lesson that learners spend working on the task set)

It is not accidental that many adults faced with a recipe book recognise, when asked, that the majority of recipes they follow are invariably illustrated. All recipes have a list of ingredients and a step-by-step description of method. Theoretically that is all that is needed. The apparent fact that most adults choose illustrated recipes draws our attention to the importance of the advanced organiser. In this example, the picture of the finished dish provides clarity about the task and with this clarity we are more confident to try the recipe.

Recent work on the functions of different parts of the brain has enriched our understanding of the importance of the advanced organiser. Right-brain learners, for example, learn the whole first and then the parts. (See Book 1 in this series, *'Accelerated Learning in the Classroom'.*) In effect, for such learners there is a preference to start with the 'big picture' and then fill in the details. For learners to embark on a piece of work without this big picture is analogous to us starting to do a jigsaw puzzle without using the picture on the box lid for reference.

In the light of this it is no mere coincidence that the assessment document for the Scottish '5 - 14 Curriculum' sets out that, *'Teachers should know the objectives for their lessons and share these with the pupils.'* Similarly for England and Wales the OFSTED Framework for Inspection pre-April 1996 states in Section 7.1, The Quality of Teaching, that teaching quality is to be judged by the extent to which teachers have clear objectives for their lessons and whether pupils are aware of these objectives.

In the current framework, Section 5.1 on Teaching requires Inspectors to obtain evidence, amongst other things, on whether pupils are clear about what they are doing, why they are doing it, how long they have to do it and the way in which they can judge success in their work.

THE QUESTION COMES FIRST

The following example is taken from a science workbook. Produced by a teacher it is fairly typical of the kind of worksheet many teachers are producing.

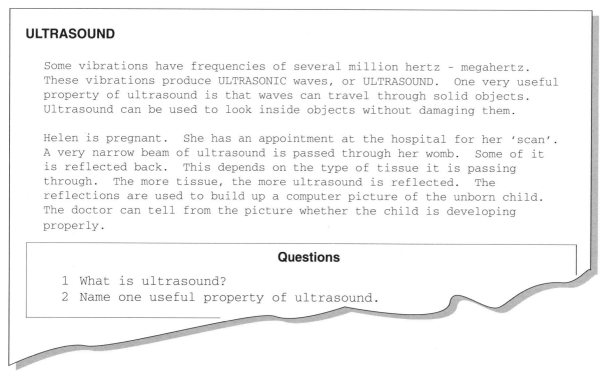

ULTRASOUND

Some vibrations have frequencies of several million hertz - megahertz. These vibrations produce ULTRASONIC waves, or ULTRASOUND. One very useful property of ultrasound is that waves can travel through solid objects. Ultrasound can be used to look inside objects without damaging them.

Helen is pregnant. She has an appointment at the hospital for her 'scan'. A very narrow beam of ultrasound is passed through her womb. Some of it is reflected back. This depends on the type of tissue it is passing through. The more tissue, the more ultrasound is reflected. The reflections are used to build up a computer picture of the unborn child. The doctor can tell from the picture whether the child is developing properly.

Questions

1 What is ultrasound?
2 Name one useful property of ultrasound.

What is typical about this example is that it contains:

- **Content information** - details about ultrasound and its uses
- **Task information** - the questions

It is also typical that the content information precedes the task information.

Read conventionally, therefore, by starting at the top, the learner reads the content and then comes to the tasks. The tasks, however, give the purpose for reading the information. By reading in this order the purpose is not clear until after the information has been read and, as a result, the information is read without a purpose. We really should not be surprised that students jump straight to the questions.

The simplest form an advanced organiser can take, results from reversing the common sequence of content information followed by task information, i.e. put the question first. This can easily be achieved.

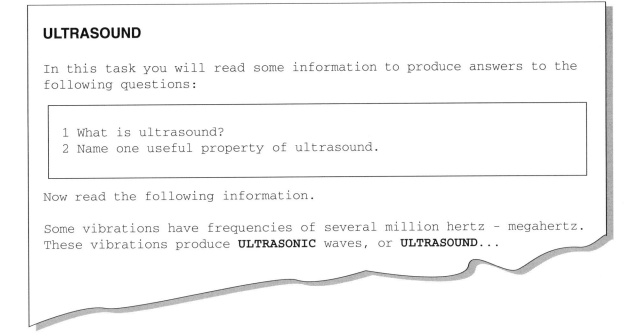

ULTRASOUND

In this task you will read some information to produce answers to the following questions:

> 1 What is ultrasound?
> 2 Name one useful property of ultrasound.

Now read the following information.

Some vibrations have frequencies of several million hertz - megahertz. These vibrations produce **ULTRASONIC** waves, or **ULTRASOUND**...

This simple idea of putting the question first can be of particular importance post-16 where there is time planned for independent private study. Without an advanced organiser and in the absence of immediate access to the teacher or lecturer, students can quickly go off task as a result of having lost sight of the purpose of their work. In the following example taken from an A Level History Study Guide on German Unification, the students can check the relevance of their research by frequent reference back to their advanced organiser.

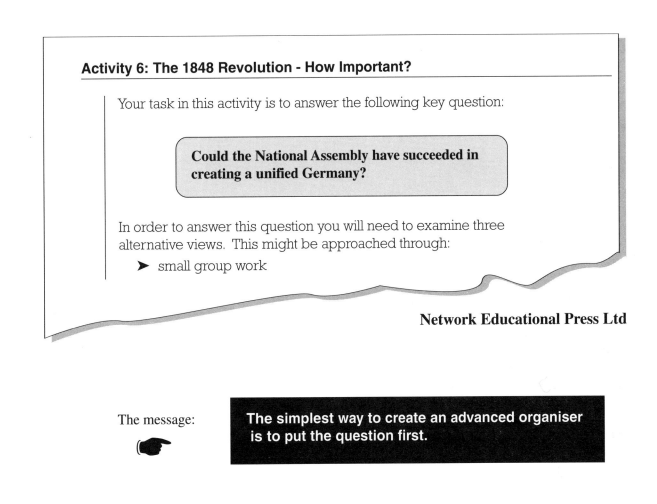

Activity 6: The 1848 Revolution - How Important?

Your task in this activity is to answer the following key question:

> **Could the National Assembly have succeeded in creating a unified Germany?**

In order to answer this question you will need to examine three alternative views. This might be approached through:

➤ small group work

Network Educational Press Ltd

The message: **The simplest way to create an advanced organiser is to put the question first.**

PUT THE SUMMARY AT THE BEGINNING

A further development to putting the question first is to start an activity with a brief introductory paragraph which outlines the activity that is to follow and which may include a statement of the purposes for it.

It could be as simple as:

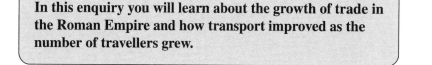

> In this enquiry you will learn about the growth of trade in the Roman Empire and how transport improved as the number of travellers grew.

Or more complex such as this example taken from a Study Guide for **Religious Education:**

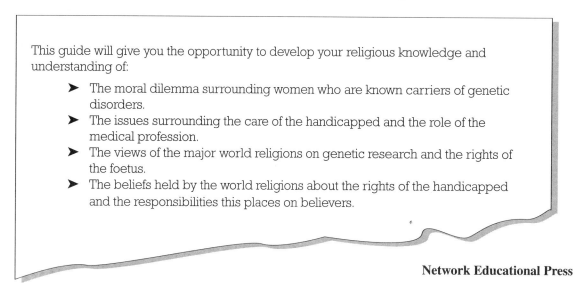

This guide will give you the opportunity to develop your religious knowledge and understanding of:

➤ The moral dilemma surrounding women who are known carriers of genetic disorders.

➤ The issues surrounding the care of the handicapped and the role of the medical profession.

➤ The views of the major world religions on genetic research and the rights of the foetus.

➤ The beliefs held by the world religions about the rights of the handicapped and the responsibilities this places on believers.

Network Educational Press

Such a paragraph, talked over and clarified by the teacher, enables students to embark on a piece of work with a clear sense of purpose and a richer picture of what has to be done. It also enables teachers and lecturers to integrate core skills in an effective and meaningful way - as in this GNVQ example:

Market Research and Consumer Trends

This guide provides opportunities to cover the following Performance Criteria:

Knowledge and Understanding:
➤ Consumer characteristics and market segmentation
➤ Green consumer spending.

Skills:
➤ Interview a supermarket manager
➤ Produce a report for future forecasting

Core skills:
➤ Communication: reports and presentations   *(COM 3.1/1/2/3/4,)*
➤ Application of number: costings, pricing   *(NUM 3.1/1/2/3/4/5/6,)*
➤ Information Technology: reports   *(IT 3.3/1/2/4,)*

The idea of creating an advanced organiser by putting a summary at the beginning can be achieved through:

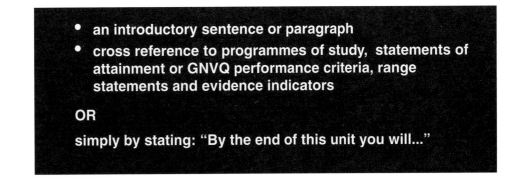

- an introductory sentence or paragraph
- cross reference to programmes of study, statements of attainment or GNVQ performance criteria, range statements and evidence indicators

OR

simply by stating: "By the end of this unit you will..."

GIVING A STRUCTURED TEMPLATE

The following example of a structured template was given out to a science class undertaking a piece of work on conservation. At a glance the student is able to see not only what will be covered, but also how the content is structured in a logical sequence. This simple sheet provides a very clear advanced organiser for the topic as well as useful white space on which the student can begin to organise his or her thoughts.

WHALES

Appearance and size of the whale	Different species of whales
How whales communicate	Whereabouts whales are hunted
Which countries hunt whales	What dead whales have been used for
Laws about whaling	Why whaling should end

The second example of a structured template was developed to help teachers on a two day Assignment Writing workshop. It provides a framework for creating activities which, through its structured nature, gives the learner a clear advanced organiser for the work to be undertaken.

STRUCTURE OF ACTIVITIES

This activity is about ...

It is important because ...

Your aim is to ... so by the end of it you should ...

You should use ... (resources; texts, CD-Rom, etc.)

You will have to produce ... (notes, diagrams, extended writing, etc.)

Your final product should include ... (guidance, hints, prompts, etc.)

You could present your work as ... (suggested formats)

Ben Walsh, Network Educational Press.

For some children, the terror created by a blank page cannot be underestimated. A structured template, by providing clarity about the task in hand, can create confidence in the learner that the task is achievable and thus overcomes the terror.

Structured templates are a particularly supportive form of advanced organiser.

PROVIDING A NOTE-TAKING MATRIX

The example given on page 19 builds on, and has all the advantages of, a structured template but also has a number of additional benefits which makes it worth noting in its own right. Designed for a group where attainment was generally low, the sheet sets out the key questions for the topic and thus provides an advanced organiser for the unit where the questions are set at the beginning. Like a template, the sheet is organised in a logical sequence so that the students have, on its completion, the notes, in paragraph order, for an extended piece of writing. In use the additional benefits became apparent:

a) the white space for recording was sufficiently small, so that note-taking had to happen rather than whole chunks of text being copied

b) prior knowledge was recorded first in pencil enabling students to build on what they knew already

c) notes from different sources were recorded in different colours of ink to promote the development of synthesising skills

On one simple sheet the teacher was able to meet a number of needs and reported that the resulting work was the best that the group had ever achieved.

Note-taking matrices are useful advanced organisers where learners have to extract and process information and can be used with a variety of sources, texts, newspapers, video, CD-Rom, television.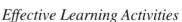

Given below are some of the important themes of the Holocaust. Try to make brief but informative notes on each.

NOTE-TAKING MATRIX

How did the Nazi's discriminate against the Jews?	How did some Jews manage to avoid detection by Nazi's?	What were the 'Ghetto's'? What were conditions like there?	Why were Jews picked on?
What were conditions like in the camps?	How were Jews transported to the camps? What happened when they arrived?	What evidence can you find of people apart from Jews being persecuted by Nazi's?	How were people killed in the camps?
When and how were the camps liberated?	What evidence have you used? Is it reliable? Do you need more?	What examples are there of people helping Jews? Why do you think German people allowed the Holocaust to happen?	What is the relevance of the Holocaust today?

MAPPING YOUR MIND

The four types of advanced organiser outlined so far have all been written examples. Tony Buzan through his work on Mind Mapping has drawn our attention to the possibility of advanced organisers for more visual learners which have the advantage, like templates and note-taking matrices, of growing with the learner's acquisition of new knowledge. In addition, by requiring the student to process the newly acquired information, they promote deeper understanding.

Mind Maps have the advantage of working like the brain works.

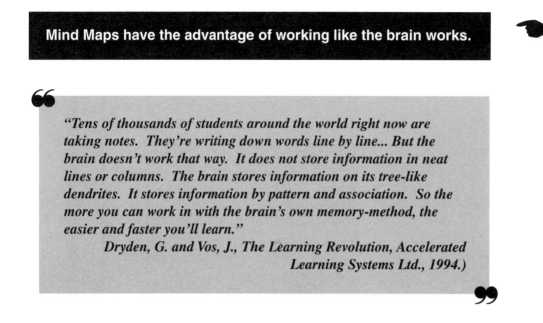

> *"Tens of thousands of students around the world right now are taking notes. They're writing down words line by line... But the brain doesn't work that way. It does not store information in neat lines or columns. The brain stores information on its tree-like dendrites. It stores information by pattern and association. So the more you can work in with the brain's own memory-method, the easier and faster you'll learn."*
>
> *Dryden, G. and Vos, J., The Learning Revolution, Accelerated Learning Systems Ltd., 1994.)*

The following example was produced by a science teacher. During the introductory lesson to a unit of work on plant growth, the class was presented with the outline of a Mind Map for the topic showing the four key sub-sections:

- Indicators of growth
- Food needed
- How food is transported
- Conditions which prevent growth

This sheet gave the learners the big picture for the topic.

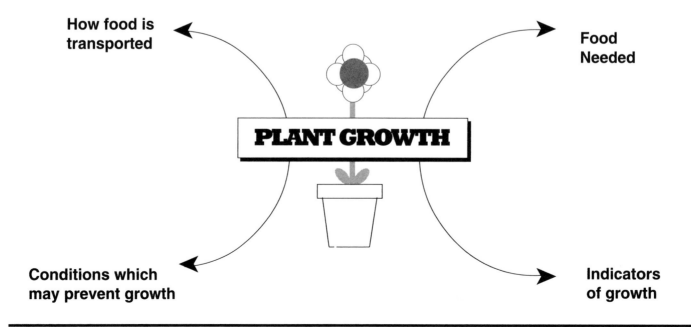

As the class worked through the topic, the students completed their own Mind Map which enabled them to record notes on the subject in a form that most helped them to memorise the details. To aid recall the students were encouraged to use as much colour and illustration as possible. New vocabulary was highlighted to further help the learners to develop the technical language of the subject.

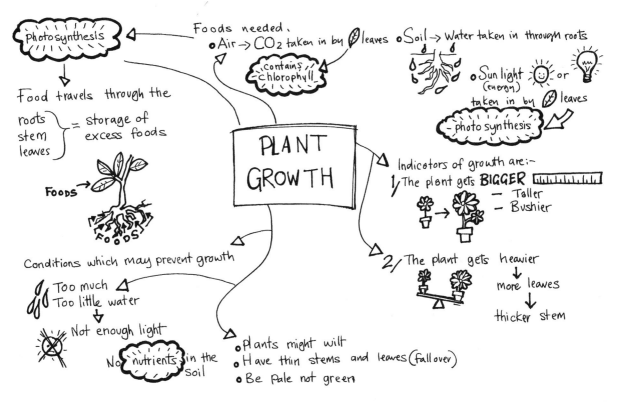

GOING TO THE FUTURE BASE

The response of some teachers to the concept of the advanced organiser is negative. They have argued that for some pupils, in particular for pupils where attainment is low, by setting out all that is to be done in advance the task looks too big. Consequently, advanced organisers are demotivating. Whilst this ignores the fact that, as we have seen, the advanced organiser can be as simple as putting the question first, there is an approach to creating the big picture which sets out from the beginning to be motivating.

Developed as a planning tool for industry and commerce, *"Future-basing is a powerful process for creating vision, deciding how to achieve it and generating a motivation to act."* (**Bill Phillips,** *'Future-Basing Explained'*, **Industrial Training Service Ltd., July 1991.**) The essence of future-basing is summarised in the following illustration included in the write-up of a two day workshop on Differentiation which made use of the technique.

Don Cole, *'Quality Learning in Lothian'*, **Issue 3, October 1994.**

At the beginning of a task we see it as a problem to be solved. We are at the foot of the staircase looking up and what we see are the risers - the obstacles we have to overcome on the way up. If, however, we imagine ourselves at the top looking downwards we see the treads - the positive achievements on the way to the top. Future-basing takes students out of the present and into an imagined future where a piece of work has been completed, so that they can see the possibility of success.

Bill Phillips argues that the benefits of the approach are that it:

a) focusses on solutions rather than problems   b) focusses on success rather than failure
c) releases creativity   d) engages both the right and the left brain
e) is motivating   f) is easy to learn and do

The four stages shown on the example that follow were applied to a piece of coursework that was to take three weeks to complete. The work started on Thursday 21st September and was to be handed in, completed, on Monday 16th October. The whole of the first lesson was taken up in future-basing.

STAGE 1
BUILD A COMPELLING VISION

The students are asked to remember something they have done which has been successful, for example, a goal scored at hockey, a race won or an award achieved and then are asked to recall how they felt at that time. Recall of what achievement feels like is particularly important and the more time spent on this the better. The teacher then states that, "It is now the 16th October and the coursework is complete and you have done it really well." The students are thus taken to the **future base** and asked to associate all the recalled feelings of success with their completed coursework. With these feelings of success uppermost, the class are asked to describe what their 'finished' coursework looks like and may start this process by choosing relevant headings, e.g. introduction, bibliography, diagrams and illustrations, evidence, presentation, etc. It is crucially important, however, that the students describe their 'finished' work in the present tense, that is as if it was indeed complete. So, "I will include a map" is incorrect whilst, "I have included a map" is correct. Being based in the future this is often the most difficult bit, but the students must be encouraged to behave as if the success has already been achieved.

STAGE 2
IDENTIFY MILESTONES

Still based in the future and still talking as if the success has been achieved, the students are then asked to identify what the major steps were in the last three weeks, e.g. "What had you done by 29th September?" This stage could be organised around individual lessons or weeks depending on what is most appropriate for the circumstances. It would also be beneficial to identify the milestones in relation to the headings set out in Stage 1, e.g. "What had you achieved in finding the information you had to get by the end of lesson 3?"

STAGE 3
BUILDING THE DETAIL

During this stage the students are asked to look at the intervals between the milestones identified in Stage 2 and outline what they had to do between each milestone. Still in the future base students 'look back' at the new information they needed and the new skills they acquired, eg "During the second week I learnt how to construct a survey into traffic congestion." It is during this stage, therefore, that the relevance of study and information handling skills becomes apparent.

STAGE 4
ACTION PLANNING

At Stage 4 the students come out of the future base into the present base and look at the previous three stages. Stage 1 has provided them with a rich picture of what they will end up with and Stages 2 and 3 with a detailed 'to do' list. As a result of the process this list is arranged in chronological order and already sorted under the relevant headings. This level of clarity about what has to be done, in what order and by when provides an excellent advanced organiser. In addition the individual student knows it is achievable because they have 'seen it'.

Whilst future-basing is time consuming it does provide a very rich and detailed advanced organiser. Investing time in the technique will, like any investment, pay dividends.

WHITE SPACE

In this section you will see that:

☞ **differentiation is not just about worksheets**

☞ **talking with the teacher is just as important if not more so**

☞ **the dialogue with the teacher can be recorded in spaces left on resources**

☞ **white space:**

- **allows work to be individualised**
- **links teaching to assessment**
- **incorporates target setting, action planning and the recording of achievement**

In *'Differentiation: a Practical Handbook of Classroom Strategies'* (**Dickinson, C. and Wright, J. NCET 1993**) a model is presented which looks at the topic under four headings:

| Differentiation by | **resource** | Differentiation by | **task** |
| Differentiation by | **support** | Differentiation by | **response** |

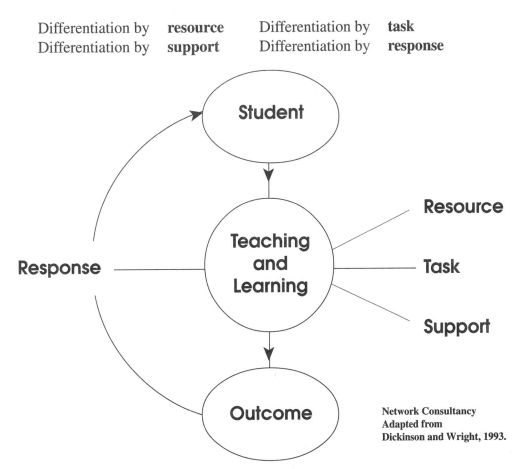

Network Consultancy
Adapted from
Dickinson and Wright, 1993.

Looked at in terms of the history of curriculum development, the emphasis from the 1970's onwards has been squarely placed on the first two categories. Generally referred to as Resource Based Learning, this approach is based on the assumption that if teachers can make content accessible through the careful design of resources, and ensure that learners are successful through the design of ability-specific tasks, then differentiation will be provided for and learning will be more effective. Such approaches have come in for much criticism.

At a practical level, resource-based strategies can result in teachers become resource technicians in their own classrooms, as the mountain of worksheets needs managing. We have all, at one time or another, been faced with a sea of hands prefacing questions such as:

> "I've finished worksheet 27 can I have 28?"
> "I need some glue."
> "Where's the Blu-Tac?"
> "My page is full. Shall I turn over?"
> "My pen's run out."

And that is only in the first 30 seconds of the lesson!

At the design stage, curriculum materials are invariably produced for three levels; hard, average and easy. Given that:

> **Most secondary schools group pupils in ability sets for some subjects... too frequently, teachers assume that pupils in such sets have exactly the same abilities, require all of them to do the same work and consequently fail to challenge the most able pupils.'**
> **(The Annual Report of Her Majesty's Chief Inspector of Schools, HSMO 1996)**

this approach to differentiation would seem to be an improvement on much current practice. When, however, we add to differences in ability other variables such as aptitude, achievement, interest, gender, ethnic origin, preferred learning style and dominant intelligence, then the three levels of worksheet becomes over simplistic.

Thirdly, it appears not to reflect what learners actually want. In *'What's the Difference? A Study of Differentiation in Scottish Secondary Schools'* (**Northern College Publications, 1993**), Simpson and Ure undertook a major survey of provision in Mathematics, Science, Modern Languages and English. The message from the learners was clear.

> **The pupils whom we interviewed were of the clear opinion that what helped them to learn - in all subjects and at all stages - was not an individualised scheme or set of resources, not a particular form of grouping or set of activities, but A TEACHER - a teacher who was readily available and approachable, who noticed when they had difficulties, who took the time and trouble to give them explanations which they were able to understand, who paced the work appropriately, who set realistic goals for them both in the short and long term, and who gave them good quality and timeous** (sic) **feedback on their performance.**

Central to learners' needs, therefore, is the role of the teacher. Borrowing from Stradling and Saunders (*'Differentiation in practice: responding to the needs of all pupils',* **Educational Research, 35, 1993**), Simpson and Ure refer to the activity of the teacher as providing 'differentiation by dialogue'.

Analogous to 'differentiation by support and response' this places the emphasis on teachers finding time to talk with learners about their work and moves us away from thinking that differentiation can only take place through resource-based approaches. Indeed, one of the conclusions from Simpson and Ure is that:

> *This, then, is the lesson for school management teams and for those whose task is to evaluate a school's educational provision - that the quality of a school's differentiation is not simply to be judged by the outward signs of doing different things with different pupils. It also poses two questions of every educational innovation:*
>
> > *Does it meet the pupils' actual and immediate needs as learners better than the present provision?*
> >
> > *Does it increase the opportunities available to teachers to identify and respond to these needs?*

In responding to these needs, teachers can increase the amount of dialogue they engage in with learners about their learning. In the busy places that classrooms are, however, the danger is that the dialogue can get lost and yet it is increasingly clear that such dialogue is crucial.

In *'Improving Schools'* (**HMSO, 1994**) evidence from OFSTED inspections is analysed to show how a number of schools have improved themselves. The case study from the secondary sector is Newall Green High School. In 1991 only 6% of the year group obtained five or more grades A to C at GCSE. By 1993, 18% were achieving five or more grades A to C representing a three-fold increase in two years. In outlining how this improvement was achieved, attention is drawn to the central importance of 'differentiation by dialogue':

> *After receiving the mock examination results every pupil has a formal interview with a senior member of staff at which they assess the marks together and set precise targets for improvement.*
>
> *Following these interviews, pupils have to arrange separate discussions with their subject teachers about how they can improve their grades. Their teachers help them to set particular learning and revision targets, and the pupils make a formal agreement to try their best to achieve them.*

In addition to this target setting dialogue at GCSE level, most pupils in most subjects in Key Stage 3 know:

a) the levels of attainment they have reached, and how they got there,

b) the levels of attainment they should be aspiring to and importantly,

c) what they have to do to achieve the levels they are aspiring to.

Dialogue with the teacher was an important feature of Newall Green's improvement in challenging circumstances.

In Section 1, we also saw the importance of this dialogue in making provision for able pupils where it was stated that such learners:

- care more about teachers comments than about grades
- want comments to be truthful, realistic and challenging
- want work to be constructively criticised
- want time to talk to the teacher

The reality, however, seems to fall short of this.

> *Children rarely received the kind of feedback on their work that helped them to know what or how to improve.*
> *(Access and Achievement in Urban Education, HMSO, 1993)*

> *Too little feedback is usually given to pupils to draw them into evaluation of their work, and teachers too rarely discuss with pupils how work could be improved.*
> *(The Annual Report of Her Majesty's Chief Inspector of Schools, HMSO, 1996)*

It would appear that we know how much is to be gained from engaging learners in a dialogue about their learning. In large measure we know what the dialogue should be about. Teachers can engage in a dialogue to:

- negotiate tasks
- support, challenge and extend
- assess and record
- set personal targets
- monitor
- celebrate achievement

On the other hand, reality suggests a picture that has less to do with discussion and more to do with worksheets. Yet the two can be reconcilled by the inclusion on worksheets of white space.

In most schools the pressure is for teachers to include as much information on worksheets as possible. This is largely a financial consideration having little to do with conditions for effective learning and much to do with the level of photocopying bills. If instead the emphasis is placed on learning then what is advocated here is an approach to worksheet design that reduces the number of words and increases the empty or white space on the page. The importance of this white space is not simply a matter of design for readability, within the context of this section, it is that the space is useable. If dialogue is important in promoting effective learning then the dialogue does need to be recorded, otherwise it is lost either between lessons or in the general busyness within lessons.

White space enables the dialogue to be recorded and thus allows teacher support and response to be incorporated within the resource. This is most clearly seen with assessment.

Teachers spend a great deal of time marking work. Generally a model is followed in which points for correction are noted in the margin, a few sentences or at most a paragraph is written at the end and then a grade or mark is given. When the work is returned, what we then hear in most classrooms is, "What did you get?" Most of the reaction by the learner is to the grade or mark and the points for improvement are largely ignored. If the work returned is coursework, it is then collected back in and kept secure for the examination board and yet on it is all sorts of important information about what the learner has to do to get better. It is in the nature of marking and assessment that crucial comments about what learners ought to be doing in the future are on work they have done in the past. The link between assessment, teaching and learning is, therefore, weak.

> **If the National Curriculum is to have its full effect on the standard of pupils' learning the connection between assessment and the planning of teaching needs to be more securely understood than has always been the case in the past."**
> **(Education Observed; The Implementation of the Curricular Requirements of ERA. HMSO, 1992)**

If, at the top of a worksheet or on the front of a study guide, teachers leave some white space then learners can use the space to transfer the targets written on the last piece of work onto the guidance for the present piece of work. In this way individual targets become part of the advanced organiser for the work. White space thus:

- allows work to be individualised without recourse to different worksheets
- enables learning and teaching to be linked with assessment
- incorporates target setting, action planning and recording achievement within one process

The value of white space is well illustrated in the following study guide for modern languages.

Clear deadlines

Teachers and students agree personal targets.

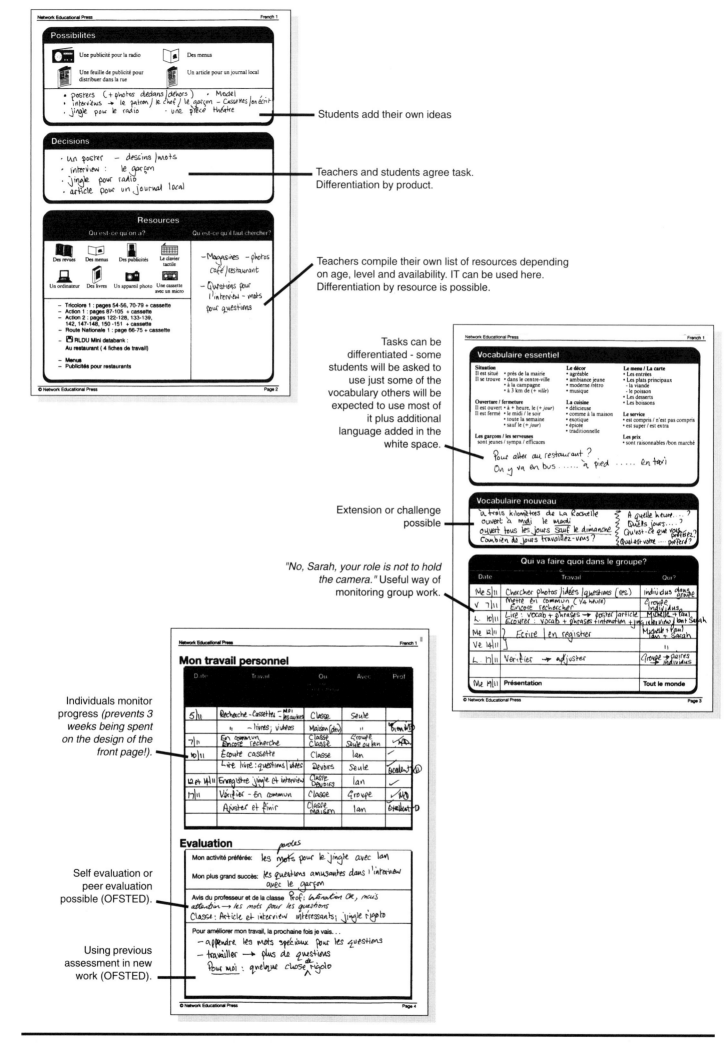

Effective Learning Activities

SEPARATE RESOURCES

In this section you will see how the separation of content from tasks:
- **saves time**
- **improves quality**
- **integrates core skills**
- **increases flexibility**
- **makes links with Resource Centres**
- **enables differentiation by resource**
- **reduces costs**

In Section 2, a distinction was made between content information and task information. In many instances resources created by teachers include both types on the same sheet of paper.

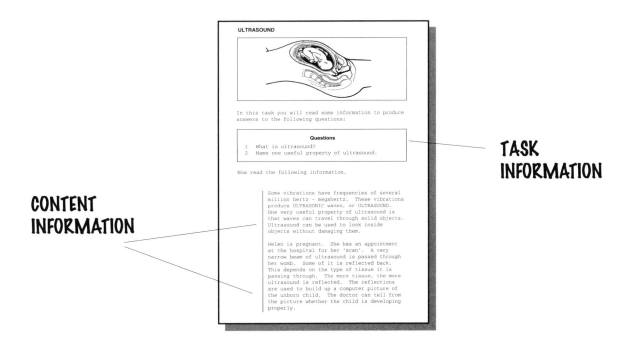

TASK INFORMATION

CONTENT INFORMATION

In the section dealing with advanced organisers, the suggestion was made that task information should precede content information. In this section we can go beyond that initial point to further suggest that the two types of information be kept separate, as in the following example.

Task card 9   **Evacuation**

```
In the war, children had to leave their homes in the cities.  They
were sent to safer homes in the country.

Choose ONE of these things to do:
  a) Draw a poster which asks people to have evacuated children in
     their homes.
  b) Write an advert which asks people to have evacuated children in
     their homes.
  c) Write a letter.  You have been evacuated.  Write a letter to your
     parents.  Tell them about your new home, what you like and what
     you miss.

Use the following resources:
  Home Front 2
  Home Front 3
  Home Front 13
```

There are seven advantages to this separation:

  1 It takes less preparation time

  2 There is no degradation in quality

  3 Information handling and information technology skills are integrated

  4 There is greater flexibility

  5 Working links are established with the Library Resource Centre

  6 Differentiation by resource is made manageable

  7 Costs are reduced

TIME

Many teachers seek, in the preparation of units of work, to emulate what publishers do. They

spend time producing both content information and task information. Often this is on single worksheets. Frequently these are combined into booklets. This involves identifying appropriate material, selecting the relevant bits, photocopying these sections, writing questions and activities and typing them up, assembling the various pieces with scissors and paste then photocopying the class set.

It is a well-established finding that, costed accurately from beginning to end, such an approach takes 10 hours of teacher time to produce one hour of student work. If teachers spend their time, energy, enthusiasm, creativity and imagination producing interesting activities to go with resources they have already got, it will take less time to construct units of work.

QUALITY

Inevitably a scissor and paste approach to curriculum development results in a degradation of quality.

The most obvious form this takes is in the loss of colour in the photocopying of the original. It can and most frequently does go beyond this to the production of ransom notes characterised by excessive font use, smudged pictures, paste-ups not square and a thin black wavy line around everything!

Produced for children who are sophisticated consumers of media, it is little wonder that they are turned off by such a diet. Again, if teachers concentrate on producing the activities that go with resources they already have, there is no degradation in quality.

INFORMATION SKILLS

Where teachers combine both content information and task information in the same document, opportunities for the development of information handling skills are limited. Much of the source material will have been partially processed before being placed in front of the learner. This removes the possibility of skill development in:

• deciding what information is needed	- *purpose, audience, form, prior knowledge*
• looking for the information	- *type, location, accessibility, appropriateness*
• selecting individual resources	- *level, accuracy, currency, bias*
• retrieving the information	- *indexes, contents, skimming, scanning, note-taking, key word searches*
• processing the information	- *relevance, completeness, analysis, synthesis.*

By separating content information from task information and concentrating on the production of the latter, teachers can promote the development of these information handling skills. This is of particular importance at GNVQ where Information Seeking and Information Handling form one of the Grading Criteria (see Section 1).

Furthermore if, in our evacuation example quoted earlier, the resource Home Front 13 is an encyclopaedia on CD-Rom or a computerised database then IT capability becomes easier to integrate into the mainstream curriculum.

FLEXIBILITY

The Resources for Learning Development Unit (RLDU), active in Bristol in the 1980's reproduced a set of postcards sent home from the trenches in the First World War.

One can imagine that such a set of resources could have valuable uses in a range of subject areas beyond history. Teachers of English, Media Studies, Art and Religious Education would, amongst many others, find the set useful.

In evaluating the impact of RLDU on classrooms it was found that significant numbers of teachers had purchased the cards and photocopied them onto worksheets alongside questions. By doing so a flexible resource had become tied to a particular set of questions. Had the two things been kept separate there would have been greater flexibility in the use of a valuable resource.

This flexibility is particularly important when dealing with new or redundant resources.

Using our evacuation example again, it is not inconceivable that these resources have to last for several years. Furthermore it is not inconceivable that a new and valuable resource becomes available during this time. One could imagine, for instance, that on a particular anniversary a local newspaper carries a reprint of a wartime edition. Dealing with this new material is problematic when content and task information is combined. Where they are separate, however, all that needs to happen is that the reprint is given a resource number, e.g. Home Front 14 and the relevant task cards amended accordingly.

However hard we try to get things right the first time, some of our resources will give rise to problems. The wording may be ambiguous or unclear for instance. We may end up throwing the resources away as redundant at the end of the unit or, due to financial pressure, make-do with what we know is second rate. It is the wastefulness of throwing away all our effort and resources that encourages us to make-do. Where tasks are kept separate from content, however, revisions are much easier and cheaper to accomplish since the content information can be kept if the task information needs revising or vice versa. Again we have achieved greater flexibility.

RESOURCE CENTRE

It is not infrequently the case that Librarians and Resource Centre Managers only become aware that the History Department is doing a topic on the Romans when the fifth child arrives at the desk to ask, "Have you got anything on the Romans?" To which the answer is invariably 'no' because the first one took the lot. As the situation develops, the History Department staff stop sending children to the Library despite the school policy on study skills because there is never anything available.

To build links with departments, however, the Librarian then circulates to departmental managers a form on which to request useful additions to the Library stock. A number of forms are returned blank on the basis that, "There is no point in ordering resources to be held centrally because they are never available when we want them." It is not difficult to see in this scenario a number of missed opportunities amongst which is the opportunity for learners to make use of a valuable asset.

The following list of examples is from a pupil guide to a topic on the Romans.

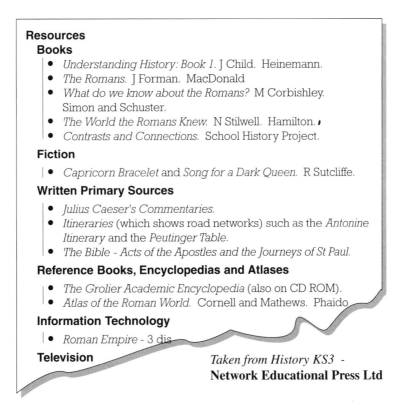

Resources
Books
- *Understanding History: Book 1.* J Child. Heinemann.
- *The Romans.* J Forman. MacDonald
- *What do we know about the Romans?* M Corbishley. Simon and Schuster.
- *The World the Romans Knew.* N Stilwell. Hamilton. *
- *Contrasts and Connections.* School History Project.

Fiction
- *Capricorn Bracelet* and *Song for a Dark Queen.* R Sutcliffe.

Written Primary Sources
- *Julius Caeser's Commentaries.*
- *Itineraries* (which shows road networks) such as the *Antonine Itinerary* and the *Peutinger Table.*
- *The Bible - Acts of the Apostles and the Journeys of St Paul.*

Reference Books, Encyclopedias and Atlases
- *The Grolier Academic Encyclopedia* (also on CD ROM).
- *Atlas of the Roman World.* Cornell and Mathews. Phaido

Information Technology
- *Roman Empire - 3 dis*

Television

Taken from History KS3 -
Network Educational Press Ltd

There is no presumption here that the learners have to use all of these resources to complete their activities. The list comprises references to possible sources of information. Furthermore, given the definition of activities outlined in Section 1, it doesn't actually matter which resource a learner uses to obtain the information.

This only matters where we set a piece of work along the lines of:

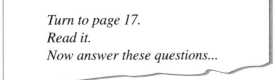

Turn to page 17.
Read it.
Now answer these questions...

With a task like this everybody needs page 17. If, however, a task is set along these lines:

This activity is about...
Your aim is to...
You should cover these points...
You can use these resources...

then it does not actually matter which of the resources the learner uses to access the information.

If it doesn't matter which resource a learner uses then single copies become useable and the Library or Resource Centre's potential can be realised. It can be realised because this approach to the separation of content from task, lessens the dependence of learners on resources that are available in the classroom, and the Resources List can be drawn up in conjunction with the Librarian to include items available in the Library Resource Centre. This joint approach also enables Resource Centre staff to be aware of the timing of units of work that require this independent research so that special short term loan and reference arrangements can be made.

DIFFERENTIATION BY RESOURCE

In the section on Library Resource Centres it was argued that through activities learners are able to make use of a wide range of resources. Inevitably the main reliance will be on the class text or texts such as in this resource list taken from a mathematics guide on co-ordinates.

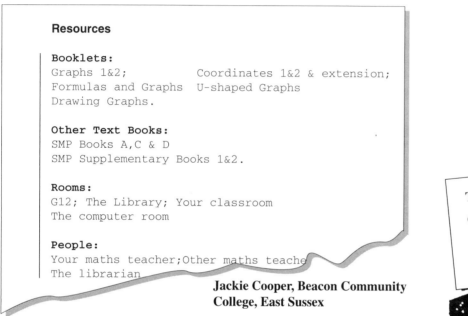

Resources

Booklets:
Graphs 1&2;   Coordinates 1&2 & extension;
Formulas and Graphs U-shaped Graphs
Drawing Graphs.

Other Text Books:
SMP Books A,C & D
SMP Supplementary Books 1&2.

Rooms:
G12; The Library; Your classroom
The computer room

People:
Your maths teacher;Other maths teacher
The librarian

Jackie Cooper, Beacon Community College, East Sussex

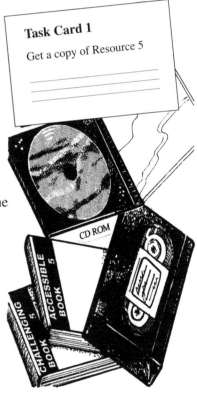

Task Card 1
Get a copy of Resource 5

The fact that this reliance is not total, however, raises the possibility of providing for differentiation by resource in a manageable way. Learners can be directed to the SMP booklet appropriate to their level or, as in the previous example, to the book on the Romans which is most accessible for those with reading difficulties, or the book which is most challenging for those who are progressing really well with the topic.

Separating content information from task information enables teachers to provide for differentiation by resource without recourse to worksheets at different levels.

COST REDUCTION

In following the argument set out above, we have seen that learning through activities rather than questions and the separation of content from tasks, enables learners to access a wide range of resources, because single copies can be used. Once it is recognised that single copy resources are useful, it is easy to draw up a resource list like the example given because, for a wide variety of reasons, departments have large numbers of single copy resources such as promotional literature from various organisations, not to mention inspection copies! If this is a possibility then photocopying bills can also be reduced because, in many departments, such bills are high owing to the need to photocopy content in large amounts.

VOCABULARY AND PROMPTS

This section looks at the importance of building vocabulary and using prompts. New vocabulary should be introduced orally, then displayed, then used.

Prompts enable teachers to:

- ☞ spend more time talking to learners
- ☞ use a wide range of support including learning support staff and other pupils
- ☞ avoid using closed questions

> " The language of school subjects often overlaps with common language and the pupil may make inappropriate connections between the two. Perhaps when new technical terms are introduced we should ask, 'What does this word mean to you?' We would then be in a position to make the use of the term explicit.
> *(K Postlethwaite, Differentiated Science Teaching, Open University Press, 1993)* "

When words have both a common and a specialist meaning, confusion can reign in learners' minds. Three examples illustrate what Postlethwaite means:

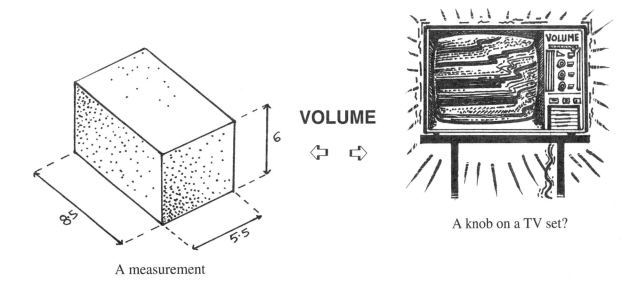

VOLUME

⇦   ⇨

A measurement

A knob on a TV set?

Player	name	score	Team	Points	Position
①	Jane	0	☆	1	10th
②	Chi	20	☐	7	4th
③	Rani	16	☐	5	6th
④	Sal	32	☆	10	1st
⑤	winston	11	☆	4	7th
⑥	Barry	6	☐	3	8th
⑦	Jill	20	☐	7	4th
⑧	Hal	22	☆	8	3rd
⑨	Davinda	31	☐	9	2nd
⑩	Jo	5	☆	2	9th

TEAMS	SCORED	POINTS	WINNER
☆	70	25	
☐	93	81	✓

A method of recording information

TABLE
⇦   ⇨

Something to put the teapot on

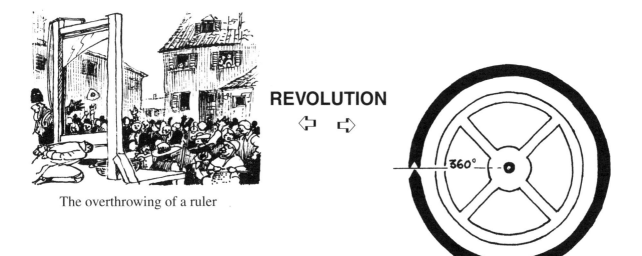

The overthrowing of a ruler

REVOLUTION
⇦   ⇨

360°

A turn of a wheel

We have all experienced trying to sort out such confusions experienced by learners. Essentially the confusions can arise either through the overlap between common and specialist language as seen above, or through the restricted vocabulary of the learner.

Teacher's question during a project on dinosaurs:
'Can anyone tell me the name of a long dead animal?'

Pupil's question in response:
'How long does it have to be?'

At best the necessity of clearing away such confusion is a drain on the teacher's time. At worst the confusion is a permanent block to the learner's understanding. The common response, especially with children who are experiencing difficulties in the subject and where emphasis is placed on success rather than success with challenge, is to remove the difficult vocabulary. Conscious of readability issues, teachers prepare information sheets at a level they perceive to be appropriate to the needs of the learner. This approach can result in a situation whereby learners with restricted vocabularies encounter content that is itself presented through a restricted vocabulary. If the learner's difficulty is, in part, the result of an impoverished vocabulary, the problem is thus compounded.

Building on the work of the Israeli Educational Psychologist, Reuven Feuerstein, the *'Somerset Thinking Skills Course'* (**Basil Blackwell, 1988**) sets out an approach to cognitive development which aims to counter linguistic deprivation. Feuerstein argued that whilst some learning results from direct exposure to stimuli, most learning is mediated by the intervention of adults. In learning theory, the starting point is with Skinner and Behaviourism. With this theory, stimulus and response are the important variables and nothing needs to be understood about cognitive functioning.

Teachers need only provide either the right stimulus or the right response.

Skinner

Piaget went on to argue that it is not enough to assume that what goes on in the learner's head is a 'black box' that we need not understand since the relationship between stimulus and response depends on the developmental level of the 'learning organism'. Thus children in the 'sensori-motor phase' need to be provided with different stimuli than students at the level of 'formal operations'.

Piaget

Feuerstein developed this by arguing that the relationship between the stimulus and the learning organism or between the organism and the response is mainly mediated by other humans. An example of this would be a parent talking to a child about putting out the milk bottles. The parent might say;

> *"How much milk do we usually get?"*
> *"Who is coming to stay tomorrow?"*
> *"How much extra milk do we need to get?"*

Here we see the parent mediating the child's learning experiences as the child operates in the environment.

Feuerstein

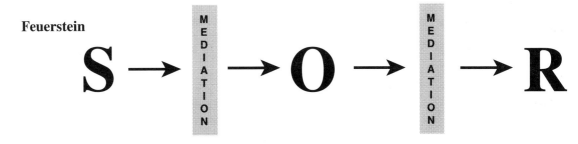

The basis for the approach, then, is that a child's interaction with the environment is usually mediated by an adult and the form that mediation takes is linguistic. Where this mediation is lacking or inadequate, children are left with an impoverished vocabulary and, therefore, are denied access to an important cognitive resource which results in limited cognitive strategies. Funded by the Low Attaining Pupils Project of the mid 1980's the Somerset Thinking Skills Course seeks, through mediated learning activities, to enable learners to think and learn about their own learning. A key feature of this is the development of language.

In Module 2: Analysing and Synthesising, an activity is given which *"Develops pupil understanding of analysing and synthesising 2-dimensional representations of 3-dimensional forms."* Teachers are given a list of key vocabulary to promote while the learners work on the activity.

With 'low attaining pupils' many teachers would avoid many of these words, confident that this avoidance would promote greater access. To avoid such words, however, is to deny opportunities for attainment to be raised. The message from the Somerset Thinking Skills Course is not to avoid difficult vocabulary, but rather to seek every opportunity to build vocabulary.

One approach to this is shown below where a preliminary activity for a unit of work sets out a framework for addressing vocabulary issues prior to commencement of the unit.

The key vocabulary list is;
- ➤ CODE
- ➤ COMPONENT
- ➤ INTER-RELATIONSHIP
- ➤ DIMENSION
- ➤ REPRESENTATION
- ➤ CONSTITUENT
- ➤ TALLY
- ➤ CHECKING
- ➤ SYSTEM
- ➤ MENTAL IMAGE
- ➤ CONCEIVABLE
- ➤ MEMORISE
- ➤ MANIPULATE
- ➤ VISUALISE
- ➤ ANALYSIS
- ➤ MODEL
- ➤ TABLE
- ➤ COLUMN
- ➤ ANTICIPATE
- ➤ HYPOTHESISE
- ➤ CONSTRUCT
- ➤ DISMANTLE
- ➤ IMAGINE

Activity 1 : Vocabulary Lists

When you find an historical term that you do not understand, record it in a vocabulary list. Explain its meaning in words and/or pictures. Ask your teacher or use dictionaries or encyclopedias to help you understand the meaning. Here is one way of doing this:

Words or Phrases	Meaning
trade	buying, selling or bartering items

Trade and Transport in the Roman Empire
Network Educational Press

An alternative approach is for the teacher to be much more proactive in the development of specialist language. Accepting that such language should not be omitted from the classroom, we can develop its use by ensuring that it is:

- Orally introduced - new vocabulary should be heard before it is seen

- Displayed around the room - vocabulary posters placed on walls above eye level to permit unconscious learning to take place through peripheral vision

- Underlined in the text with meaning given in brackets - learners can use textliners to help with this.

We can develop a sequence to employ throughout a unit of work in order to build vocabulary. The sequence is that new words should be:

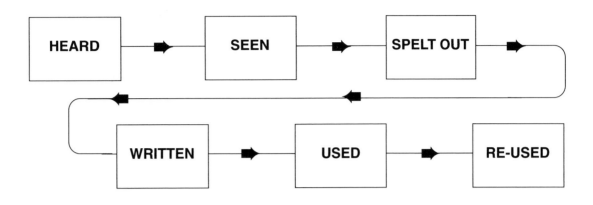

Whilst emphasis has rightly been placed on using the possibilities within activities to build vocabulary, there is one exception to this general principle. In Section 3, much was made of the importance of 'differentiation by dialogue'. This emphasised the role of the teacher in providing support and challenge as well as responding to learners' work through talk. For this to happen, teachers need time. Time can, however, be lost through the use of inappropriate vocabulary in the task information.

The following examination question appeared in 1990:

"After experimenting with various spanner lengths it was found that a long spanner was required to remove a stubborn nut. Explain the principle involved that enabled the long spanner to be successful."

For some learners the challenge in this task is in working out what the question is. There are some problem areas with vocabulary such as the use of the word 'principle' not to mention potential ambiguity with the vernacular use of the phrase 'stubborn nut'! The difficulty with the vocabulary in the language of instruction will require the teacher to mediate between the resource and the learner with the result that time to engage in dialogue is lost through having to provide remediation for inappropriate phrasing of a resource. Counter, therefore, to what has been said about building vocabulary is the point that the language of instruction, task information, should be as simple as possible, eg:

"Explain why a long spanner is better than a short spanner for removing a tight nut."

In other words, the challenge in a task should come through the performance of the task not in working out what the task is. Vocabulary should be built through performance of the task, using the sequence outlined above. The language of instruction should be kept simple to give teachers time to engage in dialogue with their learners.

The inclusion of prompts in activities plays a similar role in creating time for teachers to engage in dialogue. There is a common introduction to the study of economics that requires students to imagine that they have been shipwrecked on a desert island and to identify what they would need to survive. Being a task that requires imagination it is not suprising that, being outside the realms of most learners' experience, some students would need hints to get them started. Teachers have a ready supply of these hints:

- ✎ *"What will you do if it gets cold at night?"*
- ✎ *"How will you ensure that meat is fit to eat?"*
- ✎ *"What are our dietary requirements for health?"*

Yet these hints are invariably kept in the teacher's head, along with models, frameworks and worked examples. The teacher therefore locks him or herself into a position of being the only person in the class who can provide the help.

The argument here is that if teachers commit their prompts to paper by including them within the task information, then they will have more time to engage in dialogue with learners since they are spending less time going round giving hints. In the example below, the same introduction to economics is given, but this time prompts have been included.

ACTIVITY 1

```
In this activity you will be introduced to the study
of Economics.

By the end of this activity you should understand the
difference between:
    • necessities
    • luxuries
    • goods
    • services

You have been shipwrecked on a desert island.  You
have rescued enough food to live for two days.
In your group, plan how you will use these two days
to make sure you can still survive when the food runs
out.

You need to think about:

health    shelter      warmth
food      equipment
```

Alternatively, the prompts could be provided through a concept map.

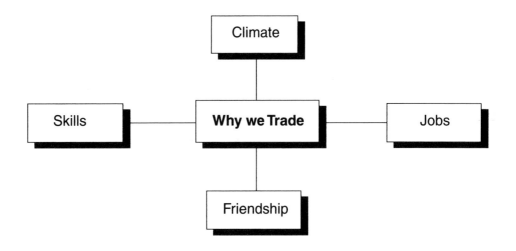

This inclusion of prompts within an activity has two further advantages. In addition to releasing teacher time to enable dialogue to take place, it allows additional support to be mobilised and reduces our dependence on closed questions.

WIDENING SUPPORT

In *'Access and Achievement in Urban Education'* (**HMSO, 1993**) OFSTED reports, in relation to in-class support, that:

> *"Joint planning with subject teachers was rare and the work of the support teacher was consequently limited to helping pupils to understand what was happening and to complete tasks. These teachers were sometimes under-occupied, during long periods of teacher exposition for example, but their presence encouraged pupils' dependence on an intermediary."*

If this is typical, it is commonplace because the reality in schools is that time for such joint planning is itself rare. Yet teachers do make use of support strategies when learners have difficulty accessing written resources. They may mobilise support from:

- special needs or learning support staff
- Section 11 staff
- parents
- and other learners (peers, senior students etc.)

However, the people providing this support are themselves not expert in the subject. The only expert in the room is the teacher. If the teacher keeps her or his expertise locked away then the teacher is the only effective source of support. If, on the other hand, the teacher's expertise is put on paper in the form of prompts, others providing support now have the information they need to make their support effective. They are in a position to say, "These are the points we need to cover." Outside the classroom also, prompts provide the librarian who is helping students with research, to know what information to search for.

In *'Classroom Management'* (**Network Educational Press, 1990**), Philip Waterhouse advocates the use of teams in active learning.

> **The benefits of the team approach soon become apparent. Questions directed at pairs or at the teams can anticipate longer, more thoughtful answers, the result of deliberation. This overcomes the main weakness of the class dialogue which can so easily degenerate into a kind of rapid fire - a succession of short questions, with one-word answers supplied by the bright and eager, and the teacher jumping from one student to another in search of the right answer. In the team approach everyone can take part, different solutions can be explored, and the students learn to justify their arguments to their fellow team members.**

This approach can be characterised as 'group support for individual work' with learners given time to discuss the task in teams prior to completing it as individuals. This gives them the opportunity to gain clarity and confidence. In the successful adoption of this strategy, the use of prompts is vital. In this instance the prompts provide the agenda for the support group discussion.

The following example from Thomas Muir High School in Dumbarton makes use of prompts to mobilise support from parents and peers. Rosemary Craig in the English Department and Debbie Queen from Learning Support worked collaboratively to create the Holiday Project. A key feature of the work was the use of Partner Prompt Learning Cards.

Group 5

Mrs Traynor and her sister Louise are taking Tom on holiday.
Tom has Spina Bifida and uses a wheelchair.

Mrs Traynor wants Tom to be able to participate in lots of activities while he is on holiday.

Aunt Louise is Mrs Traynor's younger sister and has offered to give up her own holiday to help with Tom.

Tom (13) likes to be independent and take part in many activities.

Budget
Travel and accommodation	£1500
Spending	£1500

The Holiday Proj

Activity 1

Planning Your Holiday

Using your travel and accommodation budget, work out the cost of your holiday.
Use the sheet provided to keep a note of the cost.

Remember to include
* cost per person (look for the best possible deal for children)
* insurance
* airport tax/flight supplements
* travel to and from airports, ferries, train stations
* passports

The Holiday Project

Effective Learning Activities

Partner Prompt for Learning

Thomas Muir High School

Holiday Project - Group 5
Writing a letter.

What the activity helps with

Obtaining information and advice about travel arrangements.

Thank you for your support

**Please use the back of this sheet
for any answers.**

Activity

Discuss with.........................the information and advice you would need, and where to find it, if you were travelling with a wheelchair user.

Talk about

- travel arrangements
- suitable accommodation
- facilities for people with disabilities
- addresses which may be available from the telephone directory
  library
  health centre

Partner View	Y	N	**Please feel free to comment**	Could you suggest another activity to be done at home?
Did you enjoy helping	☐	☐		
Was the activity worthwhile?	☐	☐		

REDUCED DEPENDENCE ON CLOSED QUESTIONS

The Tunisia worksheet at the beginning of Section 1 has these three questions:

- Is there a big difference between the summer and winter rain?
- In which part of the country is there the greatest difference?
- What is the difference?

We can predict the answers:

- Yes
- The middle
- Huge!

Section 1 outlined the problem with such questions. Why is it, however, that such questions are common? The main reason for this typical approach to learning through closed, didactic questions is that the writer knew what information he or she wanted the learner to acquire. The reasoning reflects Douglas Barnes's point about worksheets being based on *"an implicit distrust of children's ability to learn."*

Prompts can assist teachers in ensuring that they get the content coverage they want in the context of activities. The questions on Tunisia can be replaced by the following prompts:

Your presentation should include the following sections:

RAINFALL

- how much rain
- regional differences
- seasonal differences
- wettest and driest regions

VARIETY OF PRODUCTS

In Section 1, emphasis was placed on a 'performance' model of understanding. There appears, however, to be some evidence that some students are being asked to perform their understanding in a medium they have not mastered.

> *Teachers were usually aware of some pupils' low level of reading and spelling skills but rarely adjusted their teaching strategies to take account of this, many relied exclusively on paper and the written word when pupils would have benefited from the use of other media or from discussion.*
> **(Access and Achievement in Urban Education, HMSO, 1993)**

In this situation it is not difficult to imagine learners, with low self-esteem, complaining that they don't understand science, geography or history when the problem is not with the conceptual understanding of their subjects, but rather with the difficulty in performing that understanding. And there is a lot at stake.

> *Our evidence suggests that many children who behave badly in school are those whose self esteem is threatened by failure. They see their academic work as unwinnable. They soon realise that the best way to avoid losing in such a competition is not to enter it.*
> **(Elton Report, HMSO, 1989)**

It is possible, however, to choose a sporting metaphor that gives a greater chance of achieving success. In the high jump, the bar is set at a height at the beginning that allows all competitors to be successful and then, building on that success, the bar is gradually raised. For some students the emphasis on performing understanding in the written form sets the bar at too great a height. If the activity has options included in it as to the form the performance of understanding can take, i.e. a variety of products, then students can be directed to perform their understanding in a medium that they have got mastery of. The variety is quite wide.

PRINT BASED	ORAL/VISUAL	ACTIVE
✓ pamphlet	✓ brainstorming	✓ visit/fieldwork
✓ diary	✓ lecture/talk	✓ experiment/practical
✓ report	✓ speaker/seminar	✓ simulation/role play
✓ essay	✓ debate/discussion	✓ video/film making
✓ poem	✓ interview	✓ problem solving
✓ poster	✓ tape	✓ drama/play/review
✓ word processing	✓ radio programme	✓ work experience

Preparing a Study Guide - Network Consultancy

Two points need to be made here. Firstly, the inclusion of options about the variety of products within an activity are not options solely for the students. To do this could result in learners making inappropriate choices based on perceived easy options. Rather the choice is a guided one made in conjunction with the teacher with the purpose of ensuring that students perform their understanding in a medium they have mastery of. The white space on the activity guide can be used to record the choice made.

Secondly, the inclusion of choices is not to join a conspiracy to avoid the written word. This would further compound the problem since in public examinations understanding has to be performed in the written medium. Instead we are looking at a situation where the performance of understanding is a separate operation from putting the understanding down on paper. If the task is to describe what happens in a scene from *'Romeo and Juliet'*, some learners will be able to write that out from scratch. Others may not and as a consequence come to believe that they don't understand what happens in the scene. If, on the other hand, they are first asked to storyboard the scene as a series of cartoons, they can demonstrate that they understand and on the basis of that success are more likely to be motivated to work with the teacher to then demonstrate that success in a written form.

As well as enabling children to be successful, one can see how including a variety of products within an activity also helps us to translate our new understanding of multiple intelligences into practical classroom activities. In addition two further benefits can be identified; provision for bilingual pupils and catering for different preferred learning styles.

BILINGUAL PUPILS

In *'Assessing the Needs of Bilingual Pupils'* (**David Fulton Publishers, 1995**) Deryn Hall draws on the work of Jim Cummins to derive a framework for differentiating the curriculum for children with two languages. The model is based on a matrix with two dimensions; context and cognitive demand.

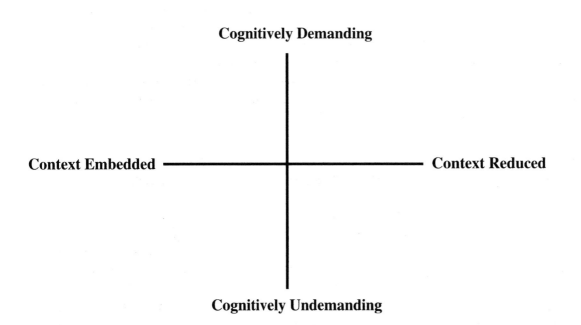

Effective Learning Activities

As the model is developed, one can see how building variety into the products required from an activity can be beneficial in planning the progression routes for bilingual students.

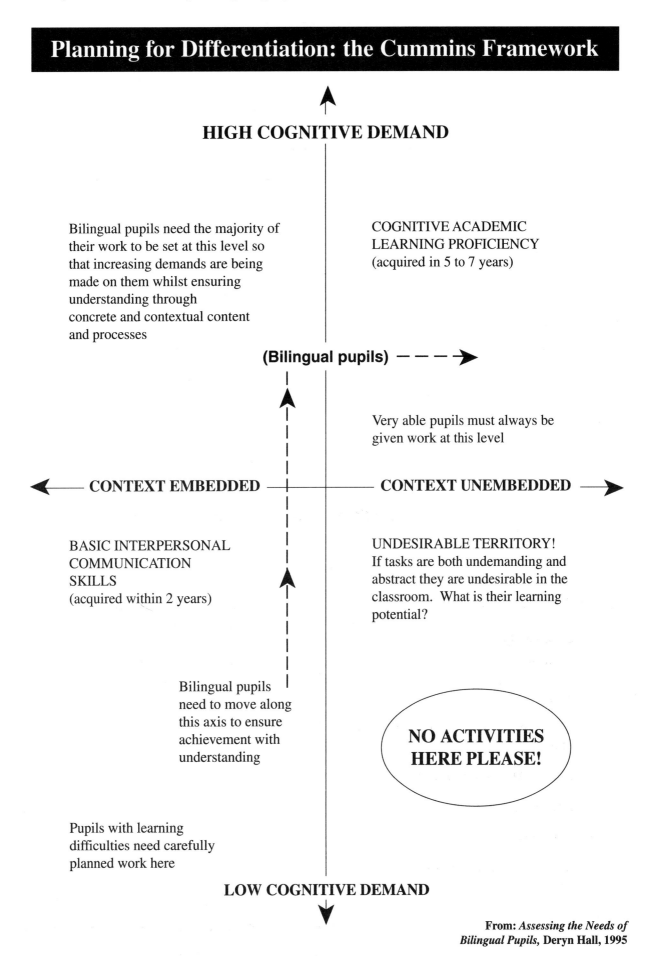

Planning for Differentiation: the Cummins Framework

HIGH COGNITIVE DEMAND

Bilingual pupils need the majority of their work to be set at this level so that increasing demands are being made on them whilst ensuring understanding through concrete and contextual content and processes

COGNITIVE ACADEMIC LEARNING PROFICIENCY (acquired in 5 to 7 years)

(Bilingual pupils) − − − →

Very able pupils must always be given work at this level

◄— CONTEXT EMBEDDED — CONTEXT UNEMBEDDED —►

BASIC INTERPERSONAL COMMUNICATION SKILLS (acquired within 2 years)

UNDESIRABLE TERRITORY! If tasks are both undemanding and abstract they are undesirable in the classroom. What is their learning potential?

Bilingual pupils need to move along this axis to ensure achievement with understanding

NO ACTIVITIES HERE PLEASE!

Pupils with learning difficulties need carefully planned work here

LOW COGNITIVE DEMAND

From: *Assessing the Needs of Bilingual Pupils,* **Deryn Hall, 1995**

Cognitive Processes: Using the Cummins Framework

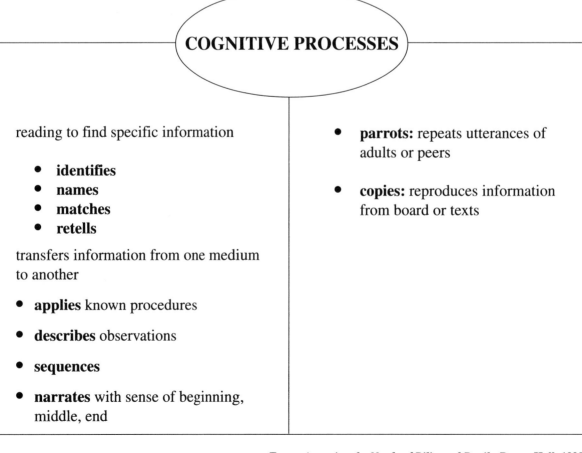

- **generalises**

- **compares** and **contrasts**

- **summarises**

- **plans**

- **classifies** by known criteria

- **transforms**, personalises given information

- **recalls** and **reviews**

- **seeks solutions** to problems

- **argues a case** using evidence persuasively

- **identifies criteria, develops** and **sustains** ideas

- **justifies** opinion or judgement

- **evaluates** critically

- **interprets** evidence, makes deductions

- **forms hypotheses**, asks further questions for investigation

- **predicts** results

- **applies** principles to new situations

- **analyses**, suggests solutions and tests

COGNITIVE PROCESSES

reading to find specific information

- **identifies**
- **names**
- **matches**
- **retells**

transfers information from one medium to another

- **applies** known procedures

- **describes** observations

- **sequences**

- **narrates** with sense of beginning, middle, end

- **parrots:** repeats utterances of adults or peers

- **copies:** reproduces information from board or texts

From: *Assessing the Needs of Bilingual Pupils,* **Deryn Hall, 1995**

PREFERRED LEARNING STYLES

In the 1980s, David Kolb developed a four stage cyclical model to explain how people learn from experience (**Kolb, D.A.,** *'Experiential Learning - Experience as the source of Learning and Development',* **Prentice-Hall, 1984**)

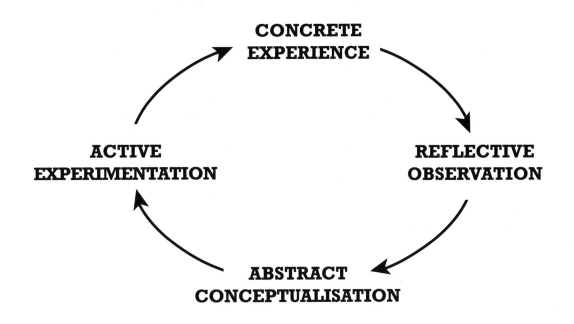

In effect, to learn from experience, we have first to think about the experience (Reflective Observation), accommodate and assimilate that with what we know already (Abstract Conceptualisation) and, on the basis of the fit or misfit with what we know already, try again (Active Experimentation) which in turn generates the next Concrete Experience.

Bernice McCarthy derived a typology of learners from this model by superimposing two dimensions onto the Kolb cycle; a vertical continuum (how we like to receive information) and a horizontal continuum (how we like to make sense of the information). This gives four learner types.

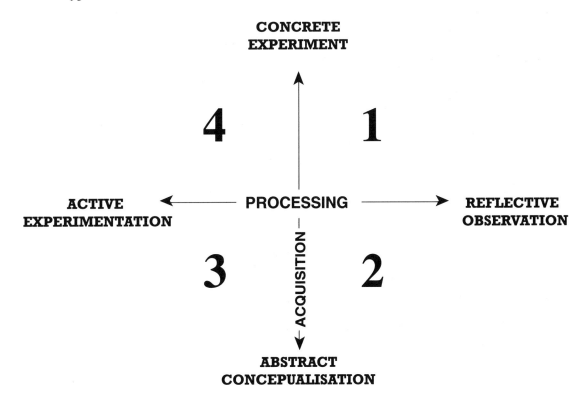

Types of Learner

McCarthy summarises the characteristics of each learner in the following way:

TYPE FOUR LEARNER

Integrates experience and application. Seeks hidden possibilities, excitement. Needs to know what can be done with things. Exercises authority through common vision. Leads by energising people. Learns by trial and error, self-discovery. Enriches reality, perceives information concretely and processes it actively. Is adaptable to change and relishes it; likes variety and excels in situations calling for flexibility. Tends to take risks, at ease with people, sometimes seen as pushy. Often reaches accurate conclusions in the absence of logical justification. Functions by acting and testing experience.

Strengths: Action, carrying out plans.

Goals: To make things happen, to bring action to concepts.

Favourite question: If?

TYPE ONE LEARNER

Integrates experience with the 'Self'. Seeks meaning, clarity, and integrity. Needs to be personally involved. Seeks commitment. Exercises authority with participation and trust. Learns by listening and sharing ideas. Values insight thinking, works for harmony. Leads by bringing about co-operation among people. Absorbs reality. Perceives information concretely and processes it reflectively. Interested in people and culture. Divergent thinkers who believe in their own experience, and excel in viewing concrete situations from many perspectives. Model themselves on those they respect.

Strengths: Innovation and imagination. They are ideas people. They function through social integration and value clarification.

Goals: Self-involvement in important issues, bringing unity to diversity.

Favourite question: Why?

TYPE THREE LEARNER

Practices and personalises. Seeks usability, utility, solvency, results. Needs to know how things work. Exercises authority by reward and punishment. Leads by inspiring quality, the best product. Learns by testing theories in ways that seem more sensible. Values strategic thinking, is skills orientated. Edits reality. Perceives information abstractly and possesses it actively. Uses factual data to build designed concepts, needs hands on experience, enjoys solving problems, resents being given answers. Restricts judgement to concrete things, has limited tolerance for 'fuzzy' ideas. Needs to know how things they are asked to do will help in real life. Functions through inferences drawn from their bodies. They are decision makers.

Strengths: Practical application of ideas.

Goals: To bring their view of the present into line with future security.

Favourite question: How does this work?

TYPE TWO LEARNER

Forms theories and concepts. Seeks facts and continuity. Needs to know what the experts think. Seeks goal attainment and personal effectiveness. Exercises authority with assertive persuasion. As leaders they are brave and protective. Learns by thinking through ideas. Values sequential thinking, needs details. Forms reality. Perceives information and collects data. Thorough and industrious, re-examines facts if situations are perplexing. Enjoys traditional classrooms. Schools are designed for these learners. Functions by thinking things through and adapting to experts.

Strengths: Creating concepts and models.

Goals: Self-satisfaction and intellectual recognition.

Favourite question: What?

From: *Education for Capability, Learner Centred Teaching* -RSA

On the basis of this typology it is possible to outline the wide variety of activities that can be used in classrooms to support different types of **learners**.

TYPE 4	TYPE 1
Open ended, problem-solving, group work	Debate
Dramatic play	Action planning
Broad brief with choices	Conversations
Presentations	Group work (structured)
Active concert	Peer teaching and learning
Work in a variety of contexts	Reflecting on performance and target-setting
Opportunities to make mistakes	Practical work
	Comprehension exercises which encourage speculation
	Opportunities to: *Hypothesise* *Ask questions* *Use imagination*

TYPE 3	TYPE 2
Problem solving	Investigations
Mentoring	Reading
Role-playing	Guest speakers
Field trips	Use of library
Making and constructing	Passive concert
Writing for an audience	Factual research
Wide variety of media: *CD* *Records* *Tapes* *Video*	Lectures
	Essay writing
	Puzzles
Variety of note-taking templates	Coursework
	Use of conceptual models
	Tests

The emphasis on variety is important. Michael Shiro's work has been adapted to identify four preferred **teaching** styles:

TYPE 4	TYPE 1
Role: Colleague **Intent of Teaching:** To enhance a better vision of what society can be. **Measure of Teaching Effectiveness:** Getting students to act upon their visions. **Purpose of Student evaluation:** To measure students' progress with respect to abilities. **Concept of Knowledge:** Knowledge gives the student the ability to interpret and to reconstruct her/his society.	**Role:** Facilitator **Intent of Teaching:** To further individual student growth according to the needs of each child. **Measure of Teaching Effectiveness:** Facilitating student growth and development. **Purpose of Student evaluation:** To diagnose student abilities so as to facilitate growth. **Concept of Knowledge:** Knowledge gives personal insights, it derives its authority from the meaning it has to its possessor.
TYPE 3	TYPE 2
Role: Manager **Intent of Teaching:** To prepare students to perform skills they will need in society. **Measure of Teaching Effectiveness:** Efficiency in getting students to achieve skills. **Purpose of Student evaluation:** To certify to clients that students have certain skills. **Concept of Knowledge:** Knowledge gives the student the ability to do certain things... capability for action.	**Role:** Transmitter **Intent of Teaching:** To advance students within the discipline. **Measure of Teaching Effectiveness:** Accuracy in presenting the discipline. **Purpose of Student evaluation:** To rank order for future advancement of the discipline. **Concept of Knowledge:** Knowledge gives the student the ability to understand certain things.

Effective Learning Activities

The danger is clear:

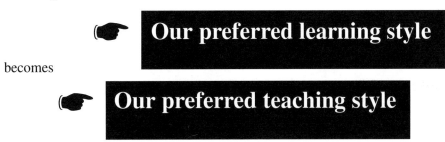

☞ **Our preferred learning style**

becomes

☞ **Our preferred teaching style**

Where this happens, learners whose style does not match with the teacher's will be 'turned off' and this could be up to 75% of the class. Not only that, but even those learners whose style does match will have their potential limited, in that effective learning should encompass approaches from all four sections of the cycle.

Including options within activities is a vital component of the model for effective learning. Providing learners with a guided choice of product, teachers can:

- enable learners to perform their understanding in a medium they have mastery of
- provide opportunities for learners to work with their different intelligences
- cater for bilingual pupils
- do justice to learners who have preferred learning styles different to their own.

GETTING STARTED

Stage 1

Identify a worksheet that:

- ✎ you commonly use
- ✎ covers an important part of the course
- ✎ could be improved

Make it realistic by selecting a worksheet that covers a small section of the course. Just two or three lessons would be a useful starting point.

Stage 2

Think of an activity that the students might do instead of the worksheet. The activity should require the learners to perform their understanding. This is where you can be creative. Define the activity in terms of a:

- ✎ purpose
- ✎ product
- ✎ audience

Stage 3

Having identified a purpose for the activity, match it to the aims and objectives of your work. You might want to think about this in terms of:

- ✎ knowledge
- ✎ understanding
- ✎ skills

It may also be possible to make a link with core skills. Aspects of cross-curricular themes could be included such as:

- ✎ experiences
- ✎ attitudes

Stage 4

Use the information from Stage 3 to create the advanced organiser for the activity. The advanced organiser could take the form of:

- ✎ putting the question first
- ✎ putting the summary at the beginning
- ✎ a structured template
- ✎ a note-taking matrix
- ✎ a mind map
- ✎ future-basing

Stage 5

Identify the resources you could use for this activity. It is important to remember that with an activity it is possible to make use of   one-off copies of books, articles, etc. List the resources under headings. Think about:

- ✎ textbooks
- ✎ information technology
- ✎ audio-visual sources
- ✎ organisations

Make links with your Library Resource Centre Manager to:
- ✎ identify relevant magazine and newspaper articles
- ✎ make arrangements for putting books on reference or short term loan
- ✎ make use of student librarians to write to relevant organisations

Make links with your IT Coordinator to identify relevant:
- ✎ software
- ✎ applications
- ✎ CD Roms

Stage 6

Design the learning activities. These should include opportunities for:

- ✎ whole class presentations
- ✎ small group work
- ✎ paired activities
- ✎ individual work

Students should be able to perform their understanding through a:

- ✎ variety of product
- ✎ variety of media

Stage 7

Identify the relevant prompts to ensure appropriate content coverage, e.g.

'Your work should include...'

List these as bullet points or diagrammatically.

Stage 8

Identify the key technical vocabulary for the activity. Produce a vocabulary checklist.

Stage 9

Wordprocess or DTP your new activity guide. Include white space on the sheet for recording:

- ✎ resources students have identified for themselves
- ✎ additional guidance from the teacher
- ✎ targets and action plans

Stage 10

Ask someone from another subject area or, better still, learning support or special needs to read your activity guidance. They are checking for:

- ✎ assumed knowledge
- ✎ vocabulary
- ✎ intelligibility

If a non-specialist can follow it easily, so will the learners.

Stage 11

Give it a go. Try it out. Learn from it, after all:

☞ *"If we do what we always did, we'll get what we always got."*

Reference Section

Resources

A selection of useful books

Ausubel, D.P.   *The Use Of Advanced Organisers In The Learning And Retention Of Meaningful Verbal Material,* Journal Of Educational Psychology, 51, 1960.

Barnes, Douglas.   *From Communication to Curriculum,* Penguin Books, 1975.

Blagg, N. et al.   *Somerset Thinking Skills Course,* Basil Blackwell, 1988.

Dickinson, C. & Wright, J.   *Differentiation: A Practical Handbook Of Classroom Strategies,* NCET, 1993.

Dryden, G. & Vos, J.   *The Learning Revolution,* Accelerated Learning Systems Ltd, 1994.

Gardner, Howard.   *Frames of Mind,* Basic Books, 1993.

Hall, Deryn.   *Assessing The Needs Of Bilingual Pupils: Living In Two Languages,* David Fulton, 1995.

Howe, Christine.   *Mix or Match,* SCRE Newsletter, 55, 1994.

HMSO   *Education Observed; The Implementation Of The Curricular Requirements Of ERA,* 1992.

Kolb, D.A.   *Experiential Learning,* Prentice Hall, 1984.

Marton, Ferenc et.al.   *The Experience of Learning,* Scottish Academic Press, 1984.

Ofsted
    i   *Access And Achievement In Urban Education,* HMSO, 1993.
    ii *Annual Report Of The Chief Inspector Of Schools, 1994 -1995,* HMSO, 1996.
    iii *Guidance On The Inspection Of Secondary Schools,* HMSO, 1995.
    iv *Handbook For The Inspection Of Schools,* HMSO, 1993.
    v Improving Schools, HMSO, 1994.

Perkins, David & Blythe, Tina. *Putting Understanding Up Front,* Educational Leadership, February 1994.

Phillips, Bill.   *Future Basing Explained,* Industrial Training Service Ltd, July 1991.

Postlethwaite, Keith.   *Differentiated Science Teaching,* Open University Press, 1993.

RSA   *Education for Capability, Learner Centred Teaching.*
                             (The Royal Society for the Encouragement of Arts,
                             Manufactures & Commerce.)

Shiro, Michael.   *Curriculum For Better Schools: The Great Ideological Debate*,
                             Educational Technology Publications, 1978.

Simpson, J.   *What`s The Difference? A Study Of Differentiation In Scottish
                             Secondary Schools,* Northern College, 1993.

Smith, Alistair.   *Accelerated Learning In The Classroom,* Network
                             Educational Press, 1996.

SOED   *Effective Primary Schools,* HMSO, 1989.

Stradling & Saunders.   *Differentiation In Practice,* Educational Research, 35, 1993.

Waterhouse, Philip.   *Classroom Management,* Network Educational Press, 1990.

White, M.   *Self-Esteem,* Daniels Publishing, 1991.

INDEX

A

able pupils, 8, 9, 26
achievement,
    celebration of, 28
    recording, 25, 29
action planning, 25, 59
activity guide, 59
advanced organisers, 13-23, 29, 57
aims & objectives, 13, 14
assessment, 4, 25, 28, 29
Ausubel, D. P., 13

B

behavioural problems, 47
behaviourism, 39
bilingual pupils, 48, 49, 55
brain, understanding of, 13
brainstorming, 47
Buzan, Tony, 20

C

choice of product, 55
closed questions, 2, 3, 37, 43, 45
cognitive processes, 50
comprehension exercises, 53
concept maps, 43
content/task information,
    separation of, 31-36
core skills, 57
cost reduction, 31, 32, 36
creativity, 6, 7, 22
critical thinking, 2, 6
Cummins Framework, 49, 50

D

debate, 47, 53
dialogue (teacher/pupil), 8, 25, 27, 28,
    29, 37, 41, 42, 43
differentiation, 1, 6 , 8, 9, 12, 25-30, 48
    by dialogue, 41
    by resource, 31, 32
    by task, 36
discussion, 12, 47
drama, 47, 53

E

enrichment, 8
evaluation skills, 2
examinations, 48
experiential learning, 51
experiments, 47

F

facilitator, teacher as, 54
feedback from teacher, 28
fieldwork, 47
flexibility in learning/
    teaching methods, 31, 32, 34
flow diagrams, 12
future-basing, 21-23, 57

G

Gardner, Howard, 6, 11-12
GNVQ courses, 2, 6, 10, 12, 33
    grading criteria, 1, 10
    performance criteria, 17
goal-setting, 4, 13
group support, 44
group work, 53, 58

I

imagination, 6, 7, 53
individual work, 58
individualised work, 25
information,
    acquisition of, 3
    organising, 14, 15, 16
    separation of content/task, 31-36
    transmission of, 10
information handling skills, 33
inspection requirements, 1
instructions, 41, 42
investigation work, 7, 53
IT Coordinator, 58
IT skills, 32, 33, 58

K

Kolb cycle, 51

L

learner types, 52
learning difficulties, 49
learning styles, 55
learning support, 37, 59
learning theory, 39
left/right brain learning, 13, 22
library, use of, 43, 53, 58

M

manager, teacher as, 54
marking work, 29
meaning making, 5
mediation of learning, 39-40
mentoring, 53
mind mapping, 12, 20, 21, 57
monitoring, 28
motivation, 21, 22, 48
multiple intelligences, 6, 11-12, 48, 55
music, 12

N

National Curriculum Council, 8
note-taking, 20, 21, 53
note-taking matrix, 18-19, 57

O

OFSTED 6, 27, 43
open questions, 3
orally based activities, 47

P

paired activities, 58
peer teaching/learning, 53
performance model, 13
performance of understanding, 47, 57
planning projects, 21-23, 25
potential, maximising, 8, 10
practical learning activities, 47, 53
preferred learning styles, 48, 51, 55
preferred teaching styles, 55
presentations, 53, 58
print based activities, 47
problem solving, 7, 47, 53
Project Zero, 4, 5, 11
prompts, 37-45, 58
puzzles, 53

Q

quality of learning materials, 33
questions, closed, 2, 3, 37, 43, 45

R

recording achievement, 25, 29
research activities, 53
resource based learning, 25, 26
resource based teaching, 27
resource centres, 31, 32, 34, 36
resources, 33, 34, 35, 58, 59
Resources for Learning Development Unit, 33
right/left brain learning, 13, 22
role play, 12, 47, 53

S

self-esteem, 9, 47
SEN Code of Practice, 8
SEN pupils, 9, 49, 59
story-boarding, 48
structured templates, 17, 18, 57
support in classroom, 43

T

target-setting, 3, 25, 27, 28, 29, 59
teacher,
    dialogue with, 8, 25, 27, 28, 29, 37, 41, 42, 43
    role of, 26
Teaching for Understanding Project, 4
teaching styles, 54, 55
team work, 44
tests, 53
time management, 31, 32, 41, 43
topics, generative, 4
transmission of information, 1, 3, 10

U

understanding,
    developing, 1, 2, 3, 6, 20
    performance of, 4, 5, 9, 10, 12, 57

V

variety in learning activities, 47, 58
visually based activities, 47
vocabulary,
    building, 40-41
    choice of, 37-45, 59
vocabulary checklists, 58

W

white space, 28, 29-30, 59
work experience, 47
worksheets, 1, 28-30, 32, 45, 57
    differentiation in, 36
    management of, 26
    preparation of, 14-16
written work, 47, 48

SCHOOL EFFECTIVENESS SERIES

Series Editor: Professor Tim Brighouse

'Effective Learning Activities' is the second title in the School Effectiveness Series, which focuses on practical and useful ideas for individual schools and teachers. The series addresses the issues of whole school improvement along with new knowledge about teaching and learning, and offers straightforward solutions that teachers can use to make life more rewarding for themselves and those they teach.

Book 1: *Accelerated Learning in the Classroom* by Alistair Smith

ISBN 1-85539-034-5

- The first book in the UK to apply new knowledge about the brain to classroom practice.
- Contains practical methods so teachers can apply accelerated learning theories to their own classrooms.
- Aims to increase the pace of learning and deepen understanding.
- Includes advice on how to create the ideal environment for learning and how to help learners fulfil their potential.
- Offers practical solutions on improving performance, motivation and understanding.

Book 3: *Effective Heads of Department* by Phil Jones and Nick Sparks

ISBN 1-85539-036-1

- Contains a range of practical systems and approaches; each of the eight sections ends with a 'checklist for action'.
- Designed to develop practice in line with OFSTED expectations and DfEE thinking by monitoring and improving quality.
- Addresses issues such as managing resources, leadership, learning, departmental planning and making assessment valuable.
- Includes useful information for senior managers in schools who are looking to enhance the effectiveness of their Heads of Department.

Book 4: *Lessons are for Learning* by Mike Hughes

ISBN 1-85539-038-8

- Brings together the theory of learning with the realities of the classroom environment.
- Encourages teachers to reflect on their own classroom practice and challenges them to think about why they teach in the way they do.
- Offers practical suggestions for activities that bridge the gap between recent developments in the theory of learning and the constraints in classroom teaching.
- Ideal for stimulating thought and generating discussion.

Book 5: *Effective Learning in Science* by Paul Denley and Keith Bishop

ISBN 1-85539-039-6

- Encourages discussion about the aims and purposes in teaching science and the role of subject knowledge in effective teaching.
- Tackles issues such as planning for effective learning, the use of resources and other relevant management issues.
- Offers help in the development of a departmental plan to revise schemes of work, resources, classroom strategies, in order to make learning and teaching more effective.
- Recommended for any science department aiming to increase performance and improve results.

Book 6: *Raising Boys' Achievement* by Jon Pickering

ISBN 1-85539-040-X

- Addresses the causes of boys' under-achievement and offers possible solutions.
- Focuses the search for causes and solutions on teachers working in the classroom.
- Looks at examples of good practice in schools to help guide the planning and implementation of strategies to raise achievement.
- Offers practical, 'real' solutions, along with tried-and-tested training suggestions.
- Recommended as a basis for INSET or as a guide to practical activities for classroom teachers

Book 7: *Effective Provision for Able and Talented* Children by Barry Teare
   ISBN 1-85539-041-8

● Describes methods of identifying the able and talented.

● Addresses concerns about achievement and appropriate strategies to raise achievement.

● Discusses the role of the classroom teacher in provision for the able and talented, and of monitoring and evaluation techniques.

● Outlines the theory, and procedures for turning theory into practice.

● Suggests practical enrichment activities and appropriate resources.

Book 8: *Effective Careers Education and Guidance* by Andrew Edwards and Anthony Barnes
   ISBN 1-85539-045-0

● Discusses the strategic planning of the careers programme as part of the wider curriculum.

● Takes practical consideration of the management careers education and guidance.

● Provides practical activities for reflection and personal learning, and case studies where such activities have been used.

● Discusses aspects of guidance and counselling involved in helping students to understand their own capabilities and form career plans.

● Suggests strategies for reviewing and developing existing practice.

Book 9: *Best behaviour* by Peter Relf, Rod Hirst, Jan Richardson and Georgina Youdell
   ISBN 1-85539-046-9

● Provides support for teachers and managers who seek starting points for effective behaviour management.

● Focuses on practical and useful ideas for individual schools and teachers.

Best behaviour FIRST AID (pack of 5 booklets) by Peter Relf, Rod Hirst, Jan Richardson and Georgina Youdell
   ISBN 1-85539-047-7

● Provides strategies to cope with aggression, defiance and disturbance

● Suggests straightforward action points for self-esteem.

Book 10: *The Effective School Governor* (including audio tape) by David Marriott
   ISBN 1-85539-042-6

● Straightforward guidance on how to fulfil a governor's role and responsibilities.

● Develops your personal effectiveness as an individual governor.

● Practical support on how to be an effective member of the governing team.

● Audio tape for use in car or at home.

Book 11: *Improving Personal Effectiveness for Managers in Schools* by James Johnson
   ISBN 1-85539-049-3

● An invaluable resource for new and experienced teachers, in both primary and secondary schools.

● Contains practical strategies for improving leadership and management skills.

● Focuses on self-management skills, managing difficult situations, working under pressure, developing confidence, creating a team ethos and communicating effectively.

Book 12: *Making Pupil Data Powerful* by Maggie Pringle and Tony Cobb

> ISBN 1-85539-052-3

- Shows teachers in primary, middle and secondary schools how to interpret pupils' performance data and how to use it to enhance teaching and learning.

- Provides practical advice on analysing performance and learning behaviours, measuring progress, predicting future attainment, setting targets and ensuring continuity and progression.

- Explains how to interpret national initiatives on data-analysis, benchmarking and target-setting, and to ensure that these have value in the classroom.

Book 13: *Closing the Learning Gap* by Mike Hughes

> ISBN 1-85539-051-5

- Helps teachers, departments and schools to close the Learning Gap between what we know about effective learning and what actually goes on in the classroom.

- Encourages teachers to reflect on the ways in which they teach, and to identify and implement strategies for improving their practice.

- Helps teachers to apply recent research findings about the brain and learning.

- Full of practical advice and real, tested strategies for improvement.

- Written by a teacher, for teachers, to stimulate thought and interest 'at a glance'.

Book 14: *Getting Started* by Henry Leibling

> ISBN 1-85539-054-X

- Provides invaluable advice for Newly Qualified Teachers (NQTs) during the three-term induction period that comprises their first year of teaching.

- Advice includes strategies on how to get to know the school and the new pupils, how to work with induction tutors, and when to ask for help.

ACCELERATED LEARNING SERIES

General Editor: Alistair Smith

Accelerated Learning in Practice by Alistair Smith

> ISBN 1-85539-048-5

- The author's second book, which takes Nobel Prize winning brain research into the classroom.

- Structured to help readers access and retain the information necessary to begin to accelerate their own learning and that of the students they teach.

- Contains over 100 learning tools, case studies from 36 schools and an up-to-the-minute section

- Includes nine principles of learning based on brain research and the author's seven-stage Accelerated Learning Cycle.

The ALPS Approach: Accelerated Learning in Primary Schools by Alistair Smith and Nicola Call

> ISBN 1-85539-056-6

- Shows how research on how we learn, collected by Alistair Smith, can be used to great effect in the primary classroom.

- Provides practical and accessible examples of strategies used by highly experienced primary teacher Nicola Call, at a school where the SATs results shot up as a consequence.

- Professional, practical and exhilarating resource that gives readers the opportunity to develop the ALPS approach for themselves and for the children in their care.

- The ALPS approach includes: Exceeding expectation, 'Can-do' learning, Positive performance, Target-setting that works, Using review for recall, Preparing for tests … and much more.

Mapwise by Oliver Caviglioli and Ian Harris

> ISBN 1-85539-060-4 Hardback
>
> ISDN 1-85539-059-0 Paperback

- Provides a thorough introduction to Model Mapping – the most powerful accelerated learning technique around.
- Illustrates how Model Mapping can be used to measure and develop intelligence and support pupils of all learning styles in increasing their essential learning skills.
- Explores the way in which Model Mapping can be used to improve thinking skills through teacher explanation and pupil understanding.

EDUCATION PERSONNEL MANAGEMENT SERIES

These new Education Personnel management handbooks will help headteachers, senior managers and governors to manage a broad range of personnel issues.

The Well Teacher – management strategies for beating stress, promoting staff health and reducing absence
by Maureen Cooper

> ISBN 1-85539-058-2

- Provides straightforward, practical advice on how to deal strategically with staff absenteeism, which can be so expensive in terms of sick pay and supply cover, through proactively promoting staff health.
- Includes suggestions for reducing stress levels in schools.
- Outlines ways in which to deal with individual cases of staff absence.

Managing Challenging People – dealing with staff conduct by Bev Curtis and Maureen Cooper

> ISBN 1-85539-057-4

- Deals with managing staff whose conduct gives cause for concern.
- Summarises the employment relationship in schools, as well as those areas of education and employment law relevant to staff discipline.
- Looks at the differences between conduct and capability, and between misconduct and gross misconduct.
- Describes disciplinary and dismissal procedures relating to teaching and non-teaching staff, including headteachers.
- Describes case studies and model procedures, and provides pro-forma letters to help schools with these difficult issues.

Managing Poor Performance – handling staff capability issues by Bev Curtis and Maureen Cooper

> ISBN 1-85539-062-0

- Explains clearly why capability is important in providing an effective and high quality education for pupils.
- Gives advice on how to identify staff with poor performance, and how to help them improve.
- Outlines the legal position and the role of governors in dealing with the difficult issues surrounding poor performance.
- Details the various stages of formal capability procedures and dismissal hearings.
- Describes case studies and model procedures, and provides pro-forma letters.

OTHER TITLES FROM NEP

Imagine That... by Stephen Bowkett

ISBN 1-85539-043-4

● Hands-on, user-friendly manual for stimulating creative thinking, talking and writing in the classroom.

● Provides over 100 practical and immediately useable classroom activities and games that can be used in isolation, or in combination, to help meet the requirements and standards of the National Curriculum.

● Explores the nature of creative thinking and how this can be effectively driven through an ethos of positive encouragement, mutual support and celebration of success and achievement.

● Empowers children to learn how to learn.

Self-Intelligence by Stephen Bowkett

ISBN 1-85539-055-8

● Helps explore and develop emotional resourcefulness in teachers and their pupils.

● Aims to help teachers and pupils develop the high-esteem that underpins success in education.

Helping With Reading by Anne Butterworth and Angela White

ISBN 1-85539-044-2

● Includes sections on 'Hearing Children Read', Word Recognition' and 'Phonics'.

● Provides precisely focused, easily implemented follow-up activities for pupils who need extra reinforcement of basic reading skills.

● Provides clear, practical and easily implemented activities that directly relate to the National Curriculum and 'Literacy Hour' group work. Ideas and activities can also be incorporated into Individual Education Plans.

● Aims to address current concerns about reading standards and to provide support for classroom assistants and parents helping with the teaching of reading.

Effective Resources for Able and Talented Children by Barry Teare

ISBN 1-85539-050-7

● A practical sequel to Barry Teare's Effective Provision for Able and Talented Children (see above), which can nevertheless be used entirely independently.

● Contains a wealth of photocopiable resources for able and talented pupils in both the primary and secondary sectors.

● Provides activities designed to inspire, motivate, challenge and stretch able children, encouraging them to enjoy their true potential.

● Resources are organised into National Curriculum areas, such as Literacy, Science and Humanities, each preceded by a commentary outlining key principles and giving general guidance for teachers.